D1395583

FIRST
WORLD
WAR
FOLK TALES

FIRST WORLD WAR FOLK TALES

HELEN WATTS & TAFFY THOMAS

The History Press

First published 2014

The History Press
The Mill, Brimscombe Port
Stroud, Gloucestershire, GL5 2QG
www.thehistorypress.co.uk

© Helen Watts & Taffy Thomas, 2014

British Library Cataloguing in Publication Data.
A catalogue record for this book is available from the British Library.

ISBN 978 0 7509 5832 5

Typesetting and origination by The History Press
Printed in Malta by Gutenberg Press Ltd.

Contents

Acknowledgements

Illustrations by Steven Gregg.

'Only Remembered' traditional English version by John Tams, lyrics reproduced by permission of John Tams. 'Old Brown' based on a traditional rhyme told to us by Albert 'Nabs' Smith. 'The Rushbearing' by William Wordsworth (1770–1850), written in 1815 – out of copyright. 'Saint Oswald's Day' hymn words by Canon Hardwicke Drummond Rawnsley (1851–1920). 'Strange Meeting' by Wilfred Owen (1893–1918), written in 1918 – out of copyright. 'War' (Rhyfel) by Ellis Evans (1887–1917), translated by Alan Llwyd for *Out of the Fire of Hell: Welsh Experience of the Great War 1914–1918 in Prose and Verse* (Gomer Press, 2008), reprinted by permission of Alan Llwyd. The story of Gilbert Insall based on the original text 'Gilbert Stuart Martin Insall and Thomas Ham Donald' (from the archive Tales of the VC) from

www.europeana1914-1918.eu/en/contributions/
5375#prettyPhoto – Creative Commons Attribution-
Share Alike 3.0 Unported licence (CC BY-SA 3.0).
'The Photo of the Girl I Left Behind Me' song lyrics
written and composed by Billy Merson (1881–1947).
'The Girl I Left Behind Me' traditional folk song also
known as 'Brighton Camp', lyrics first published in
Skillern's Twenty Four Country Dances for the Year 1799
by Thomas Skillern, derived from the traditional song
'The Girl I Left Behind Me', lyrics first published in
The Charms of Melody, Dublin, Ireland, issue no. 72,
printed in Dublin from 1791. 'It's A Long, Long
Way To Tipperary' by Jack Judge (1872–1938)
and Harry Williams, written in 1912. 'In Flanders
Fields' by Lt Col John McCrae (1872–1918), written
in 1915, first published in the *Punch* magazine in
December 1915.

Every effort has been made to contact copyright
holders of material reproduced in this collection but,
where this has not been possible, the authors would
like to apologise for any cases of unintentional copyright transgression and would like to hear from any
copyright holders not acknowledged.

Prologue

Only Remembered

Fading away like the stars in the morning,
Losing their light in the glorious sun,
Thus would we pass from this earth and its toiling,
Only remembered for what we have done.

Only the truth in the life we have spoken,
Only the seed that in life we have sown,
These shall pass onwards when we are forgotten,
Only remembered for what we have done.

Who'll sing the anthem and who'll tell the story,
Will the line hold will it scatter and run,
Shall we at last be united in glory,
Only remembered for what we have done?

Traditional English / John Tams

Introduction

THE GREAT WAR OF 1914–18

War has always played a powerful part in the story of our country's history. Every battle, every campaign – from Hastings to Culloden, from the Crimean to the Falklands – has its own story and each has something to teach us about our relationships with our fellow human beings, about our ambitions and our dreams, our strengths and our weaknesses, and our capacity for love and for hate.

But of all the wars which have affected our nation, it is perhaps the Great War of 1914–18 which has left the biggest mark … and it truly was a 'great' war. Never before had so many nations, from all over the globe, come up against one another at the same time; never before had armed forces of such numbers clashed on so many fronts and on so many battlefields; and never before had the impact of a war been so powerful. More than twenty-seven countries, including men and women from Britain's colonies all over the world, took part in the war and by the end of it more than 16 million people were dead (about half of those being civilians), another 21 million had been wounded, and the balance of power in Europe – as well as the country borders which formed the European map – had been shifted completely.

One hundred years on, as we remember what happened during those four long years, the First World War continues to stir up strong feelings. We are shocked by the millions of lives which were lost and it is hard not to question the tactics chosen by the generals who, from behind the safety of their desks in their headquarters, made decisions which so often put the lives of men fighting on the front line at risk. We find it hard to believe that so much of the war was fought out of filthy, mud-ridden trenches – and that soldiers could be stuck there for months on end, thousands of them dying in order to advance just a few metres into enemy territory. We find it difficult to understand how wave upon wave of troops could be sent 'over the top' to their deaths – hundreds of soldiers at a time being ordered to climb out of the trenches and advance straight into enemy fire across no-man's-land.

Yet while the First World War was horrific, brutal and bloody, it was also crucial in terms of stabilising Europe, redefining the European map and preventing any one country from becoming too powerful. It was a fight for democracy in which Britain and her Allies (and then the United States of America when they joined the war in April 1917) were battling against the autocratic, military threat being imposed by Germany and Austro-Hungary, which also brought about the downfall of Tsarist rule in Russia. Crucially, for Britain, it was a fight for liberty and those who survived it were proud to be part of a nation which had defeated its enemy by pulling together and standing firm.

TALES FROM THE GREAT WAR

People remember their history as stories, recounting their experiences, their feelings, their hopes, fears and dreams in tales sometimes written down and often shared by word of mouth. The stories they choose to pass on are a restatement of our cultural identity and can reveal more about the feelings of folk than any history book.

When 'the last fighting Tommy', Harry Patch, died at the age of 111 in 2009, there were those who feared that this also meant the demise of the tales from the First World War trenches. They could not be more wrong, for folk tales have a life of their own, giving them a unique kind of immortality. Thousands of stories, told both during the years of 1914–18 and after the conflict had ended, have survived as fragments entrusted to relatives in spidery handwriting in letters home and remembered through oral anecdotes, such as those shared when grandchildren discover an old tin hat or a gas mask.

These are just slivers, precious scraps of information linking decades and generations. However, with love and care, Helen Watts (an experienced author and editor) and Taffy Thomas (a storyteller who has spent his life immersed in folklore and popular culture) have worked to reconstitute these shards into retellable tales for the current and future generations of historians and storytellers.

The diaries and the letters home reveal the narrative of the struggle and something of the feelings of those who were there in the trenches. The poetry and the songs from the popular entertainment of the day – music halls and variety theatres – reveal something of the feelings of relatives and survivors on the Home Front. All are included in this unique collection.

As you absorb the tales of heroic men and women who changed the course of history, remember that their diaries and their stories show that most of them didn't consider themselves unusual or heroic; just ordinary folk who answered the call. Cling to the words of George Bernard Shaw, who commented:

War does not decide who is right but who is left.

One

Legends of the Fallen

THE ROCK CLIMBERS

*The English county of Cumbria has a long history
of legend and folklore. Its beautiful, often wild and
rugged landscape, with Lakeland as the jewel in its
crown, is not surprisingly a natural source of inspiration for storytellers and writers. This was certainly
the case in Victorian times, when Lakeland became
a popular destination and place of residence for poets
and storytellers like the great William Wordsworth,
John Ruskin and Beatrix Potter. However, it was
also during this period – a time when adventure
and exploration was very much encouraged – that
Lakeland also became a venue for a new recreational
sport: that of rock climbing. The following story from
the early twentieth century is proof that these two
Cumbrian passions – mountaineering and creating
and telling stories – did not suddenly cease with the
end of the eighteenth century and the onset of the
Great War.*

In the years leading up to 1900, two young men
loved to test their skill, strength and courage
together on the rock faces that grace the likes of
Scafell, Skiddaw and Helvellyn. With the start of the
First World War, Lord Kitchener pointed his finger
and one of the pair answered the call, heading for
France, Belgium and the horrors of trench warfare.
His friend continued on his days off to rock-climb,
although it had become a lonelier and more dangerous activity, as any solo climber knows.

One sunny day, after a particularly tough route on Scafell Crag, he was walking down a gully known as Hollow Stones, when he heard a cheery whistling. He was delighted to see the smiling face of his soldier friend coming towards him, presumably home on leave, going up to do the same route he himself had just conquered. They chatted of what they might do when the war was over. Then, parting, the pair agreed to meet up later at the Wasdale Head Inn for a pint.

The soldier never showed up for that drink. A couple of days later, the climber heard that his friend had fallen at Passchendaele, at exactly the time they had met in the beautiful sunshine of a Lakeland summer.

THE HARTEST FLORINS

On the Sunday nearest to 11 November every year, people gather at war memorials to remember the dead of the two world wars. There is probably a war memorial somewhere near to you, and if so you will know that war memorials usually take the form either of a statue of a soldier, or of a column of stone engraved with the names of the dead. However, if you were to go to the war memorial in the village of Hartest in West Suffolk, you wouldn't know you were at a war memorial unless you had read or heard this story.

For a start you'd be in the bar of The Crown, the village pub! If you investigated the room carefully, you might just spot some coins nailed to a wooden beam: twenty-four florins and a farthing to be exact. Even without any names to accompany them, these coins are this village's war memorial. This story explains why.

In 1914, the men of the village of Hartest – and the boys who looked old enough to pass as men (and boys often did pretend they were old enough) – volunteered to join the British Army.

The night before these brave young men left to go to war in France and Belgium, they took their mothers, wives and girlfriends for a drink in the village pub. As they said their sad farewells, each woman nailed a coin to the beam, telling her man that when he returned home safely, he could take that coin to buy enough food and drink to have a week's rest before returning to work on the farm. (Amazingly, a florin – worth about ten pence – would have done that, a hundred years ago.) The one woman who couldn't afford a florin nailed a farthing (a quarter of an old penny).

Thankfully, if you visit this place today and look closely at the same beam, you will see that there are more holes in the wood than there are coins, one for every soldier who returned. But the fact that there are twenty-five coins remaining shows that, even in that small village, there were twenty-five good men who never returned to their families – a sad but true story.

———

The late Albert 'Nabs' Smith – a Suffolk forester from the village of Chillesford near Orford – regaled Taffy Thomas on many occasions with the following rhyme as they supped Adnams Ale in the bar of his sister Vera's pub in Butley, The Oyster Inn.

Old Brown

Old Brown sat in the Rose and Crown
talking about the war.
He dipped his finger in the froth and
then began to draw.
These are the Allied lines he said,
and this is the German foe.
The potman he called time.
Old Brown shouted Whoa!
Do you want us to lose the war?
Do you want us to lose the war?
To call time now it would be a sin,
Another two pints we could have been in Berlin!
Do you want us to lose the war?

BILLY PEASECOD'S HARP

Since the seventeenth century, the people of Grasmere, Cumbria, have picked rushes from the lake, decorated them with wild flowers and paraded them through the village to St Oswald's church on Rushbearing Day. The Grasmere parish magazine of 1890 describes the bearings as follows:

> The rushbearings are varied in device; simple poles, crosses, hearts, wreaths are all common and among others have been wont to appear a tall pole with a serpent twisted about it, a little Moses in the bushes and a harp, designs which probably at one time conveyed scripture lessons or bore witness to some old legend.

Over the years the custom has attracted many different visitors and followers, one of whom was William Wordsworth, who wrote the following passage about the Rushbearing in 1815:

The Rushbearing

Closing the sacred Book which long has fed
Our meditations, give way to day
Of annual joy one tributary lay;
This day, when forth by rustic music led,
The Village children, while the sky is red
With evening lights, advance in long array
Through the still churchyard each with garland gay,
That, carried sceptre-like, o'ertops the head
Of the proud bearer. To the wide church door,
Charged with these offerings which their fathers bore
For decoration in the Papal time,
The innocent procession softly moves:
The spirit of Laud is pleased in the Heaven's pure clime,
And Hooker's voice the spectacle approves.

William Wordsworth (1770–1850)

The following short tale centres on a Grasmere lad who took part in the Rushbearing before going off to war.

William 'Billy' Warwick Peasecod was born in 1898. As a boy he became a member of the church choir at Grasmere's parish church, St Oswald's. Like most of his friends, Billy participated in the Rushbearing processions, carrying a bearing year after year, throughout the first decade of the twentieth century.

However, Billy's bearing was very different from all the others. As he was of Irish descent, it was decided that the local carpenter should create for him a new bearing in the shape of the harp of David. Billy's mother then decorated the intricate wooden structure with rushes and flowers, rowing out far on to Grasmere Lake to collect lilies.

For several years Billy proudly carried his harp in the Rushbearing. But then, in 1915, one year into the Great War, he joined the Border Regiment as a signaller. His regiment was posted to France where, on 5 November 1917, Billy was killed, aged nineteen.

No one could face carrying Billy's harp in the Rushbearing after that, and it fell into disrepair. However, for the Millennium Rushbearing, Billy's successors in the O'Neil family invited the local carpenter to make a replica of Billy's harp. The bearing was decorated once again with lilies, and was carried in the parade that year by Terry and Sarah O'Neil.

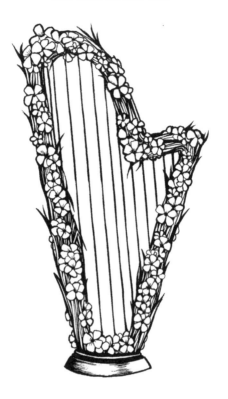

As the procession passed by Taffy Thomas' famous Storyteller's Garden in the centre of Grasmere, this story of Billy and his harp was told in his memory.

Each and every year, as they celebrate Rushbearing Day, the people of Grasmere pause their procession at the village green in order to sing the following hymn:

Saint Oswald's Day

Today we come from farm and fell,
Wild flowers and rushes green we twine,
We sing the hymn we love so well,
And worship at Saint Oswald's shrine.

The Rotha streams, the roses blow,
Though generations pass away.
And still our traditions flow,
From Pagan past and Roman day.

Beside the church the poets sleep,
Their spirits mingle with our throng,
They smile to see the children keep
Our ancient feast with prayer and song.

For saintliest king and kingliest man
Today our 'burdens' glad we bear,
Who with the cross Christ's war began
And sealed his dying wish with prayer.

We too have foes in war to face,
Not yet our land from sin is free,
Lord, give us Saint Oswald's grace
To make us kings and saints to Thee.

Our garlands fall, our rushes fade,
Man's day is but a passing flower;
Lord, of Thy mercy send us aid
And grant Thy life's eternal dower – Amen.

Canon Hardwicke Drummond Rawnsley (1851–1920)

THE STRANGE MEETING

Arguably one of the most famous names associated with the First World War is that of poet Wilfred Owen. Born near Oswestry, Shropshire, in 1893, Owen joined the British Army as a volunteer in October 1915 at the age of twenty-two. He experienced trench warfare and would have understood how horrific conditions could be on the front line in those narrow, cramped ditches, which were often deep in water, mud and snow. Owen also saw the terrible results of poison gas attacks and himself suffered both physical and mental injuries. After a period in a Scottish hospital, recovering from shellshock, Owen returned to the war. In October 1918, he won the Military Cross for the bravery he showed in taking a German machine-gun post and using the gun he had captured to kill enemy soldiers.

It was these brutal experiences which influenced much of Owen's writing and which undoubtedly coloured his view of the war. Once a proud, enthusiastic volunteer, he became one of the war's most outspoken critics.

The following story is based on an entry in the diary of Harold Owen, Wilfred's younger brother, who was a naval officer serving on board the HMS Astraea *which had been sailing the South Atlantic off the coast of Africa. It was during this time that Harold contracted malaria.*

The diary entry in question was written in the days following the Armistice. It is not impossible that the severe fever which can accompany this life-threatening disease caused Harold to suffer the hallucination which he recounts, but his description of it is lucid and, even if his vision was brought about by a temporarily disturbed mind, its timing was nonetheless remarkable.

O n 11 November 1918, the day peace was finally declared, Harold Owen, a British naval officer, was on board ship, moored off the coast of Cameroon. His thoughts, however, were thousands of miles away on the Western Front, where his older brother, the poet Wilfred Owen, had been fighting. Harold wondered how his brother would be celebrating the long-awaited news of peace and he looked forward to seeing him again when they were both back home in England.

When the red African sun had sunk behind the horizon, Harold went down to his cabin to write some letters. As he drew aside the curtain which separated his bunk from his fellow officer's, he was shocked to see Wilfred sitting in his chair, his brother's khaki field dress looking strangely out of place on board a navy ship.

The stunned but overjoyed young officer asked his brother how he had got there, but Wilfred replied only with a smile. Confused, Harold repeated his question a second time, but again Wilfred remained quiet, and again he answered with only a smile.

Harold was so happy to see his brother after so many months of separation that, rather than continue with his questioning, he accepted Wilfred's silence and sat down on his bunk, turning away as he did so to remove his cap and lay it on the blanket beside him. When he turned back to look upon his brother once more, the chair Wilfred had been sitting on was empty.

Overcome with sadness, Harold lay down on the bunk and soon fell into a deep slumber. When he woke a few hours later, he did not need to turn his eyes to the chair beside him. He knew that it would be empty, for he had woken with the certain knowledge that his brother Wilfred was dead.

Although Harold had received no official communication, Wilfred Owen had indeed been killed in action far away in Northern France. On 4 November 1918, in the final week of the war, he had been shot dead while crossing the Sambre-Oise Canal.

———

Knowing that Harold Owen claimed to have seen his brother's ghost in his cabin on board ship, it is uncanny that Wilfred himself wrote the following famous poem in which the ghost of a fallen soldier appears to another.

Strange Meeting

It seemed that out of the battle I escaped
Down some profound dull tunnel, long since scooped
Through granites which Titanic wars had groined.
Yet also there encumbered sleepers groaned,
Too fast in thought or death to be bestirred.
Then, as I probed them, one sprang up, and stared
With piteous recognition in fixed eyes,
Lifting distressful hands as if to bless.
And by his smile, I knew that sullen hall;
By his dead smile, I knew we stood in Hell.
With a thousand fears that vision's face was grained;
Yet no blood reached there from the upper ground,
And no guns thumped, or down the flues made moan.
'Strange friend,' I said, 'Here is no cause to mourn.'
'None,' said the other, 'Save the undone years,
The hopelessness. Whatever hope is yours,
Was my life also; I went hunting wild
After the wildest beauty in the world,
Which lies not calm in eyes, or braided hair,
But mocks the steady running of the hour,
And if it grieves, grieves richlier than here.
For by my glee might many men have laughed,
And of my weeping something has been left,
Which must die now. I mean the truth untold,

The pity of war, the pity war distilled.
Now men will go content with what we spoiled.
Or, discontent, boil bloody, and be spilled.
They will be swift with swiftness of the tigress,
None will break ranks, though nations trek from progress.
Courage was mine, and I had mystery;
Wisdom was mine, and I had mastery;
To miss the march of this retreating world
Into vain citadels that are not walled.
Then, when much blood had clogged their chariot-wheels
I would go up and wash them from sweet wells,
Even with truths that lie too deep for taint.
I would have poured my spirit without stint
But not through wounds; not on the cess of war.
Foreheads of men have bled where no wounds were.
I am the enemy you killed, my friend.
I knew you in this dark; for so you frowned
Yesterday through me as you jabbed and killed.
I parried; but my hands were loath and cold.
Let us sleep now …'

Wilfred Owen (1893–1918)

THE BLACK CHAIR

This story is adapted from a tale given to us by singer and storyteller Kathy Wallis. It tells of a young shepherd who lived near the village of Trawsfynydd in North Wales, and who became a national hero. The shepherd's name was Ellis Evans and, as well as tending sheep, the young man was also a talented poet. He was so talented in fact, that in 1917 he was awarded the Chair for Poetry and Storytelling at the National Eisteddfod of Wales – an annual celebration of Welsh culture and heritage. Evans' name was called out three times at the ceremony before it was sadly announced that the poet would not be able to collect his award, for he had been killed in the fighting at Passchendaele. So the chair was draped in a black cloth before being presented, instead, to his parents. The chair still exists and is on display for visitors to see in the poet's former farmhouse home of Yr Ysgwrn.

High up in the hills of the Snowdonia National Park lies the small Welsh village of Trawsfynydd. It is a beautiful place. If you go there in the morning, you can see the sun coming up over the hills, drenching the valleys with gold. If you go there in the spring, you can see how the colours change from the harsh, dark browns and greys of winter to the fresh, green colours of spring. That's the time when the sheep go back up the mountains, and with them go the shepherds.

If you had been on those same mountain slopes in spring just over a century ago, you might have seen one particularly talented young shepherd herding his sheep down the track and up into the hills to graze. He knew all the best places. He had learned from his father, along with his brothers. It was in his blood. Oh, how that young shepherd loved to sit up on the mountain and look down into the valleys. He said it gave him inspiration … and it did. He took the colours, the greens, the purples, the reds and the golds, and he wove them into pictures painted with words.

The shepherd's name was Ellis Evans, and he was the eldest of eleven children. It was not always easy being the eldest of so many children; sharing a small cottage with all his siblings and both parents on an isolated hill farm. Ellis was given daily chores to do, as well as being asked to help look after the sheep.

In the mornings, Ellis would get up early and help his mother and father get the house ready for the day. He would fetch the water from the well and the wood for the fire, then he would help his brothers and sisters to get up and dressed. And when all this was done, he had to walk the mile or two down the lane to the elementary school where he was taught his letters and his numbers.

Most of the time, Ellis was a good lad, but sometimes he would be accused of daydreaming. He wasn't really daydreaming; he was conjuring – conjuring pictures in his head and weaving them into words.

By the time he was eleven years old, Ellis was already composing beautiful poems and his teachers spotted in him a real talent. He wasn't so good at his numbers, or his geography or his history, but when it came to words, Ellis shone.

Now, the Evans family was a very Christian family and every Sunday without fail, whatever the weather, the whole family would walk down to the chapel in the next village, walk back home again for a bite to eat and then walk back to the chapel a second time for the evening service.

To the young Ellis, the sermons seemed to go on for ever, and sometimes he'd be told off for fidgeting and not paying attention. He didn't always want to hear what the vicar was saying either. His sermons were all hell, fire and brimstone, designed to warn the congregation – and especially the children – of all the dreadful things that would happen to them if they were not good in the eyes of God.

Hearing the vicar's words, young Ellis was truly afraid and shook to his boots. But as soon as the sermon had finished and the hymns began, his heart would rise up once more, full of joy. The words of those hymns wove the pictures back into his life, and once again his ideas would flow.

Back then children didn't stay on at school as long as they do today, and Ellis was just fourteen years old when, armed with what he'd learned at school and in the chapel, he set off on the next stage of his life. From then on he went to work all day and every day on his father's farm, tending the sheep.

As he sat up in the mountains and on the hills, the colours, the pictures and the words all spun round his head and he began to write. At the end of the day he would come down off the mountain and read his poems to his friends and neighbours in the village. Listening to the beautiful words, the villagers could see the pictures exactly as Ellis had seen them in his head: the beauty of the land, the beauty of the valley, all conjured into beautiful verse.

Sometimes Ellis would talk of religion, and his poems would retell the stories that he had learned in chapel. Sometimes his poems would be about nature, reflecting the beauty of the Welsh landscape which formed his very own part of heaven here on earth.

Ellis was just nineteen years old when he entered the local Eisteddfod. He did not win, but to him taking part was pure joy. He found that he loved performing his poems and the people loved his performances. Wherever Ellis went, the people would come to hear him. They would hold their breath as he took to the stage and marvel at the beauty, the romance; his pictures of nature woven into words.

They knew him not as Ellis Evans, but as Hedd Wyn or 'Blessed Peace'. They say Ellis chose the name one morning as he watched the sun cutting through the mist in the valley below him as he tended the sheep.

As the years passed, Ellis' poems took on a maturity. He mastered his craft, and his poems were a thing of wonder.

And so it was that he decided to write a special poem – a poem in praise of Wales' highest peak, Snowdon. It was a poem of beauty and Ellis was proud of it – so proud, in fact, that he entered it in the National Eisteddfod of Wales.

Once again, Ellis' poem did not win the coveted chair, and although everybody loved it and wanted to hear more, this wasn't good enough for our Ellis. He was determined that one day the chair would be his; one day it would be his poems, his pictures woven in words, that would earn him the National Chair.

But dark days were to come. People's lives were turned upside down. The evil in the darkness began to spread, from one country to another, across the world. The people of Trawsfynydd didn't think that a war across the sea would harm them or touch them in their little village halfway up the mountain, but eventually it did. The days would still dawn bright, the sheep would still need tending and there were still poems to write, but now the whole country needed their help.

The men from the Ministry came to visit and demanded that the farmers grow extra food, raise extra sheep. Then the men from the parliament in London said that all the young men had to join the war. The men from Trawsfynydd and thousands of villages like it began to march away, leaving the women and children behind.

Then the messengers began to arrive. One after the other they would come, bringing news of yet another life ripped from this earth – a friend, a relation, gone for ever.

And so the weeping began. Those left behind wept enough tears to water the earth. They wept enough tears to make the crops grow in a barren year. And all the time they wept, their young men and boys marched away to become shadows in their memory.

It was a dark morning when Ellis marched away from his village. It seemed the war wasn't going to plan. So many of the young men who had first been claimed by the government were being sense-lessly slain in the mud of Belgium, that they came for the rest. Among them was Ellis.

What pictures must have been going through his head as he walked away from his beloved mountain, from his beloved valley, and away from his beloved home! No more pictures of beauty. No more pictures of romance. For Ellis was going to a world where green had turned to brown, where fields had turned to quagmire, and in the place of the peaceful sounds of sheep, birds and water tumbling over the rocks, came the sounds of gunfire and bombs. Trees that once had green leaves touching the earth now stood as stark trunks, bereft of branches. The beauty that had enshrined Ellis' life was wrenched away and he was plunged into a world of terror and mud and blood.

Ellis was lucky at first, and after his training, he was allowed home for two precious weeks of leave. Back in the warmth of his farmhouse kitchen, he sat at the table and wrote and wrote – the shocking experience of his time at war pouring onto every page. Ellis did not stop until fourteen days had turned to twenty-one and he had turned from a soldier to a deserter. There was a knock on the door and Ellis was marched from the hayfield to the prison, and then from the prison straight to the muddy trenches of Passchendaele as a Royal Welsh Fusilier.

Amid the mud and the bloody gore of the Belgian battlefield, Ellis finished the poem he had begun back on the kitchen table in the cottage in Trawsfynydd. He signed it with the pseudonym Fleur de Lys, and on the day his completed poem was sent back to Wales, he marched to the Battle of Passchendaele.

Ellis was crossing Canal Bank at Ypres when a nosecap shell cut him down. As blood seeped from his stomach, he fell to his knees, grabbing the earth with his hands. Desperately trying to save him, the stretcher bearers ran quickly to his side and carried him to the first aid post, but it was too late. After asking the doctors, 'Do you think I will live?', Ellis drew his last breath and died.

When the name Fleur de Lys was called out as the winner at the National Eisteddfod that year, the trumpets sounded but no one stepped forward to claim the chair. The trumpets sounded a second time but again no one stepped forward. Then, for a third and last time, the trumpets blew, before the archdruid stood and solemnly announced that the winner, the mysterious Fleur de Lys, had been killed in action just six weeks before. The empty chair was draped in a black sheet and the archdruid proclaimed, 'The festival in tears and the poet in his grave'.

The black chair was then carried all the way to the mountains of Snowdonia and to Ellis' parents' farmhouse in Trawsfynydd. And there it remains, to this day, for everyone to see so that, instead of a legacy of death and mud and blood, people can celebrate the legacy of the mountains, the valleys, the sheep and the babbling stream that Ellis loved: the beauty of this life.

War (Rhyfel)

Why must I live in this grim age,
When, to a far horizon, God
Has ebbed away, and man, with rage,
Now wields the sceptre and the rod?
Man raised his sword, once God had gone,
To slay his brother, and the roar
Of battlefields now casts upon
Our homes the shadow of the war.
The harps to which we sang are hung
On willow boughs, and their refrain
Drowned by the anguish of the young
Whose blood is mingled with the rain.

Ellis Evans (1887–1917)

Translated by Alan Llwyd for Out of the Fire of Hell:
Welsh Experience of the Great War 1914–1918 in
Prose and Verse *(Gomer Press, 2008), reprinted by
permission of Alan Llwyd.*

Two

*Supernatural
Sightings*

It is not surprising that young soldiers, suddenly exposed to the very real possibility of dying in a foreign land, felt scared and more than a little confused. This combination of fear and confusion could lead to dreamlike delusions. So it was that the rumour ran from soldier to soldier the length of the front line, that soldiers facing defeat and death had unmistakably seen a wispy white figure beckoning them to safety if they followed him. The figure became known as the Angel of Mons, named after the Belgian city near to where a key battle took place. Countless sightings of the Angel were reported back to family and friends in Britain. Here follows a selection of those legends.

THE ANGELS OF MONS

The first few days of August 1914 were crucial for the future of the German Empire. Having declared war on Russia on the first day of that month, the Kaiser was very aware that France, who had a treaty with Russia, might retaliate. For Germany, being geographically sandwiched between these two hostile nations was worrying as it meant there was a very real possibility of facing a war on two fronts at the same time. The only solution, so the Kaiser and his generals believed, was to nip one problem in the bud as quickly as possible.

Predicting that it would take Russia longer to mobilise its troops, the Kaiser drew up his Schlieffen Plan, central to which was the decision to attack France first – and swiftly – and to neutralise them before facing the mighty Russia in the east. But the Kaiser made one assumption too many. The King of Belgium was not going to allow German troops to pass through his country en route to Paris without challenge, and refused to give in to the Kaiser's demands. So, on 3 August 1914, Belgium faced the reality of a German invasion.

Stepping up to defend their Belgian allies, Britain immediately issued the Kaiser with an ultimatum to end hostilities but, when no withdrawal came, it was Britain's turn to declare war. By 22 August, 100,000 British Expeditionary Force (BEF) soldiers had crossed the English Channel and four infantry divisions and one cavalry division were headed for Belgium. Just one day later, on 23 August 1914, they were fighting their first major battle on the Western Front – the Battle of Mons.

The battle proved to be an unforgettable start to the Great War for the British. The aim was to try to hold back the German Army and keep it from advancing into French territory. However, the German Army proved to be far stronger than the BEF expected; outnumbering the British troops by more than two to one. Without the support of their French allies, who were already rushing back to defend their capital city, the British found themselves in danger of being surrounded and, under heavy attack, were forced into a rapid retreat.

There seems little doubt that the bloodiness of this first battle shocked the British, who were clearly not expecting to be so overwhelmed in their first major engagement. Equally, there seems little doubt that the British Government realised the damage to morale that *this could have caused – not only among the troops but also among civilians back home in Blighty. So when stories began to emerge of angels appearing on the battlefield at Mons, holding back the Germany army and thus helping British soldiers to retreat unharmed, they are unlikely to have resented the suggestion that their troops were ultimately in God's protection.*

This is the tale of the first of these stories and how it evolved into one of the most famous First World War legends of all time.

In 1910, a forty-seven-year-old Welsh writer with a passion for horror, fantasy and mystery, took up a post as a journalist on the popular London newspaper, *The Evening News*. His name was Arthur Machen, and although his new job saw him writing – far more frequently than before – about factual matters, he never lost his love of legend and folk tale. For a long time, Machen had been intrigued by the legends of King Arthur and ancient stories of the Holy Grail, and he had spent many years searching for grains of truth within these romantic stories of kings and queens of old, brave knights and beautiful maidens, lost religious practices and ancient Christian beliefs. But even successful creative writers can struggle to make a living so, to secure a steady income and thereby a good home for his wife and baby son, Machen knuckled down and got on with the day-to-day grind of working as a newspaper journalist, while continuing to write fiction whenever he could.

Machen was soon to have plenty of new inspiration for his writing for, in 1914, he reported on his country's descent into war, and right from the start, there came back from the trenches tale after tale of great deeds and immense bravery amid bloodcurdling horror. For journalists like Machen, extracting the fact from the fiction in each of these tales was not always easy. The noose of censorship was pulled tight, as the British Government tried to control the news which leaked back to home shores. So when rumours reached Machen's desk of a surprise defeat and a rapid retreat from the Allies' first major engagement on the Western Front at Mons, Machen may not have known for certain where the truth stopped and the gossip began. What he did know was that his country was in danger of spiralling into panic and fear. The people needed, he believed, a story that would inspire them and restore their self-belief.

So he put pen to paper and he wrote a story about a soldier in the midst of a battle, in which his side was outnumbered and under constant artillery attack but in which he was saved by heavenly intervention. He submitted the story to his editor for placement in *The Evening News*, cleverly choosing the feast of Saint Michael and All Angels – 29 September – as its publication day. He named the story 'The Bowmen', and it went something like this …

This is the story of the retreat of the 70,000, relating to 70,000 of the 100,000 or so brave soldiers who made up our British Expeditionary Force at the start of this Great War. It is a gruelling and a terrible tale of a moment when our men faced far worse than just heavy losses; they were in danger of being wiped out altogether.

Among the brave young men going into battle that day was a young soldier from London. After days of marching south, he and his battalion had reached the front line, where a great German army had gathered and was trying to push its way onto French soil. As night approached, they dug themselves a thin line of trenches along the banks of a moss-green canal, hoping that its slow-moving waters would offer some protection when the fighting began.

At first light the next morning, the soldier and his companions awoke to find the landscape cloaked in a thick blanket of mist. Barely able to see their hands in front of their faces, they knew that any attempted attack on the enemy was sheer folly. So they watched, and they waited, certain that when the time came to fight, they would be victorious.

Eventually, as the sun climbed higher in the sky, it burned off the morning mist and, peering over the edge of their trenches, the British were able to see for the first time the scale of the enemy they faced. Even the most battle-hardy swallowed hard, trying not to lose faith as it became clear that they were outnumbered at least two to one.

But the soldiers had little time to dwell on their fears as, at that instant, the German artillery barrage began and, thick and fast, a torrent of shells rained down on the British trenches from higher ground. The ground burst open, bodies were ripped apart and the blood ran thick into the mud. Then in the wake of the artillery barrage came a second attack, this time at ground level, as hundreds of German infantry poured across the canal's narrow bridges, some even clambering across lock gates to get closer to their enemy.

At first the machine gunners and rifle men posted along the British front line held firm and blasted away at the approaching enemy, but for every grey-coated stampede which stumbled and fell, another would replace it. The British were being overwhelmed.

Morning turned into afternoon and the Germans now began to surround their enemy. One by one, the British guns were silenced and the Germans sniffed their first whiff of victory. Their soldiers came crashing down into the British trenches. At once brutal and bloody, the gruelling battle raged on.

The young Londoner, who had never stopped firing his gun, paused for a moment and turned to shake hands with the soldiers lying in the ditch beside him. As he looked into each pair of eyes, he could see the hope draining away as each prepared himself for the end. As he turned back to his gun and began to fire once more, one of his comrades started to sing, his voice dull and flat as he adapted the words to his favourite song:

It's a long way to Tipperary, it's a long way to go.
It's a long way to Tipperary, to the sweetest girl I know!
Goodbye Piccadilly, Farewell Leicester Square!
It's a long, long way to Tipperary, And we shan't get there.

Hearing the names of his beloved London streets, the young soldier suddenly remembered a small vegetarian restaurant which he had not long ago discovered and which served a delicious dish of lentil and nut cutlets. But, as hungry as he was, it was not the memory of the flavour of that meal, nor its mouth-watering aroma which now filled his mind – it was the plate upon which it was served. He distinctly remembered the picture and the lettering painted upon it: a picture of Saint George, dressed all in blue, accompanied by the words *Adsit Anglis Sanctus Georgius*.

'May Saint George be a present help to the English,' he whispered, translating the Latin. Then he spoke the motto again, this time louder as he fired his gun; then louder again, screaming the words in defiance as he blasted away, firing everywhere … anywhere … slamming bullets into the bodies of his approaching enemy.

Then suddenly, tears streaming down his face, he stopped, for a shudder ran up his spine and his skin turned icy cold. Everything around him seemed to fall silent and still, and he could see his breath, heavy on the night air. Then he heard a voice, booming out across the battlefield. 'Array, array, array!' it cried. 'Saint George for merry England.'

The young soldier looked up and to his amazement a shaft of bright light suddenly penetrated the night sky, like sunlight creeping through a great tear in a blackout curtain, and the battlefield was illuminated in a ghostly glow.

Then, floating down the beam of light, came a host of silver-white angels, dressed as archers and carrying golden bows and arrows. Like the mist which had hovered over the canal that dawn, the angels floated above the ground between the two armies' lines, forming a silvery safety net around the remaining British soldiers.

The soldier stood in awe, rooted to the ground as he watched one angel raising its hand and pointing at the enemy. Then the entire army of angels opened fire, showering the Germans with shimmering arrows, pinning them back so that the British soldiers could make their retreat.

The young soldier and his companions fled, only slowing to an exhausted trudge when the cries of battle behind them had completely faded away. No one spoke a word. Those who had witnessed the heavenly vision were unsure whether or not to believe what they had seen. Had Saint George really brought his Agincourt bowmen back from the dead to help the English in their hour of need? Meanwhile, others kept shaking their heads as if trying to clear their minds of a temporary madness. Most were too traumatised by the scale and the speed of their defeat in the battle to utter a sound. Some were so tired that they slept as they walked.

Back on the battlefield, some 10,000 Germans also slept, but theirs was not the sleep of the exhausted; it was the sleep of the dead. Yet as they moved among their fallen men, the Kaiser's generals could find no blood, no wound, no mark of any kind on their bodies.

———

Machen never claimed that 'The Bowmen' was anything but a fictional story and he never mentioned Mons within it nor named any soldier

on either side. However, the style in which he wrote the tale was so believable that the readers of *The Evening Times* became convinced that it was based on eyewitness accounts.

Frustrated when Machen repeatedly denied that there was any grain of truth in his tale, his critics then accused him of a deliberate attempt at a hoax. It seemed that nothing Machen could say would make any difference. His story had become a legend and had begun to run away from him.

As it was repeated, précised and retold, the legend of the phantom bowmen grew and evolved, sometimes becoming more fantastical, at others being increasingly locked into reality. And gradually, as the Great War went on, the Angels of Mons began to give birth to other folk tales. Men returned from battlefields far and wide with reports of strange sightings, spiritual encounters and tales of ghostly apparitions. Only one person appeared to tire of the mysterious legend and prayed that he would hear it no more: the man who had created it and unleashed it upon the world – Arthur Machen.

AN ANGEL'S GUIDING LIGHT

The Coldstream Guards are probably Britain's most iconic infantry regiment. One of seven regiments within the Queen's Household Division, they are the soldiers famous the world over for the bright red tunics and tall, bearskin caps which they wear for ceremonial duties like the Trooping of the Colour and the Changing of the Guard at Buckingham Palace. However, it is the guards' lesser-known skill – their adaptability for rapid deployment to a wide range of duties – which makes them one of the most courageous and disciplined regiments of the British Armed Forces.

When Britain entered the First World War in 1914, the Coldstream Guards were among the first troops to cross the Channel to France, and they fought in some of the most famous and bloody battles. The regiment suffered devastating losses in the First Battle of Ypres in October 1914 and also played a key role at Mons, at the Somme, Loos, Ginchy and again at Ypres in 1917.

The following tale was first told by British-born writer Arch Whitehouse, a frequent contributor to the 1920s pulp fiction, aviation adventure story magazine Flying Aces. The story was published in Whitehouse's book Heroes and Legends of World War I in 1964, fifty years after the event which inspired it is deemed to have taken place. Although told as if based on a reported account from eyewitnesses, Whitehouse's story contains no real names. This, and his penchant for exaggeration, has led many to dismiss the tale, and the ghostly vision described within it, as pure fiction. However, who knows what those exhausted and traumatised soldiers of the Great War battles might have seen or imagined at a time of such great stress, fear and emotion? Might dreams have felt like reality? Might hallucinations have seemed tangible? Whatever the truth behind Whitehouse's legend, the soldiers he describes encountering the angel certainly seemed to live a charmed life during the hours, days and weeks which followed the Battle of Mons.

It was in the early hours of 24 August 1914 when Field Marshal John French gave the order for the great British retreat from the Battle of Mons to begin. Thousands of soldiers joined the march, exhausted, heads hanging; some mourning the loss of comrades and others stumbling under the weight of the battered and torn bodies of the wounded. Among those who were the last to leave was a company of the King's own Coldstream Guards. Staying true to their reputation for courage, discipline and loyalty, these brave infantrymen fought on, protecting the rear of the retreating force long after others had fled.

Yet their courage was to bring them no instant reward, for when a safe moment finally came for them to leave their posts, the guards found themselves lost and alone. Separated from the rest of their battalion, they had no idea which way to march and no certainty of catching up with their retreating comrades.

What's more, night was approaching. The guards knew that to wander on blindly through the dark was pure folly, so they decided to halt and make camp for the night. Their best chance of survival, they knew, was to dig themselves a trench and wait until dawn, when they could continue the search for the rest of their regiment.

Anxious that the enemy would more than likely have followed them, the soldiers took turns to stand guard while others tried to catch a precious few moments of sleep.

Now, the eyes and the ears can play tricks in the dead of night, and it was while the second watch was on duty (a few minutes after midnight) that one young soldier, peering out over the edge of the trench, spotted a bright light just a few feet away. The light flickered and then disappeared, before suddenly reappearing, brighter this time and swaying gently from side to side.

Surprisingly, the young soldier was not afraid. The light was coming from the opposite direction to that in which the guards had marched, so his first thought was not of the enemy.

'Must be someone messing about with a flashlight,' he muttered to himself, before calling out, 'Who's that out there? You'll get yourself shot, you darn fool!'

There was no reply. Instead, the light drew closer.

Anxious now, the young guard readied himself to fire. He opened his mouth, preparing to shout 'Halt or I'll shoot,' but his words caught in his throat, for as the light grew brighter, he saw that it was beginning to take a human shape … a female shape … a tall, slender woman dressed in a long, flowing robe of white. On her head was a thin, golden crown and springing from her shoulders were two delicate, snow-white, feathered wings.

Amazed, the young guard dropped his weapon and began to shake his companions from their slumber. As each man awoke, the guard pointed to the angelic vision over his shoulder.

One by one, the men gathered themselves, swallowing hard and blinking as their startled eyes tried to fathom the true nature of the luminous shape. Mouths agape, they wondered if they were truly awake or if they were still dreaming.

The angel was now standing on the very rim of the trench, and as she looked down at the men huddled below her, she smiled and her hair fell softly forwards around her face. Still she did not utter a word, but when all the men were awake, she lifted her hand, gesturing that they should follow her.

The young soldier who had been on guard immediately bent to pick up his gun and made ready to obey the angel, but his companions held him back, nervous, suspecting a trick.

'She means us no harm,' said the young guard. 'She has been sent to guide us. Come, we should have faith. We should follow.'

The soldier appeared so calm and so certain of the angel's protection that his companions' doubts were eased, and one by one they followed the ghostly figure out of their makeshift trench. Keeping their heads low, they followed the angel across a muddy field, she appearing to drift effortlessly over it while their mortal feet stumbled after her through the dark.

The angel led them to a sunken lane: a perfect, sheltered escape route from any pursuing Germans. The men were able to move more swiftly now, on firmer ground, and they made good progress, following in the angel's silent footsteps.

When they came to the end of the lane, the angel led them out of the gully and up a steep bank. At the top of the bank, she halted and turned to face the soldiers, smiling once again. Raising a slender hand, she pointed to a small wood nearby. Before the men could question her meaning, however, she vanished; her light snuffed out in an instant like a candle in the wind.

Not knowing what else to do, the men headed into the wood, thankful that the angel had led them to a safer place to see out the night. But they soon realised that she had done much more than that, for camped among the shelter of the trees and watching them approach, was the rest of their battalion.

The next day, at daybreak, the soldiers told their comrades about the angel and how she had helped lead them to safety. Most of them laughed, joking that the soldiers had succumbed to the madness of Mons, but a small group of those with more faith agreed to accompany the guards and retrace their steps, to see if their experience had indeed been true.

The men made their way out of the wood and down the steep hill. The young soldier and his companions from the previous night were all certain of the direction in which they had wandered. But try as they might, not one of them could find the sunken lane along which they had been led by the angel. Nor could they find it on any map. Like the angel, the lane had simply vanished.

Whether or not the Guards' heavenly visitation had been real, the angel had certainly led this brave group of men to safety. She had blessed them with good fortune, too, for those same Coldstream Guards travelled on from Mons to Ypres. There, once again, they found themselves isolated and fighting alone to defend a dangerously exposed position. Yet somehow, against all the odds, they held that post, without support, for more than twenty long days.

THE VISION OF THE VIRGIN

Echoing the many legends featuring protecting angels and heaven-sent visions, which grew out of the fighting on the Western Front, is this legend from a Prussian town called Suwalki on the Eastern Front. Today, Suwalki lies in north-eastern Poland, but before the map of Europe was redrawn under the terms of the 1919 Treaty of Versailles, these parts of Polish land were under the control of, firstly, the Russian Empire and then, after 1915, the German Empire.

The legend features a Russian captain, who was leading the army that was invading Eastern Prussia near the start of the war, in an attempt to overthrow German control. The source of the story is said to be a Russian general, under whose command the captain served. It is possible that this is General Pavel Rennenkampf, who chased the Germans out of the area around Suwalki for nine days in the Battle of Augustovo, which took place from 26 September to 9 October 1914.

At the start of the Great War, the generals of the Russian Army had a problem. They needed to strike quickly and hit out at their German enemy while it was at its weakest and while large portions of German troops were tied up in the invasion of Belgium and France.

Yet the Russians could not advance too far into German territory to the west without first protecting their own flanks. For to the south was Galicia, where a huge Austro-Hungarian force awaited, and to the north was the kingdom of East Prussia. Here lay the seat of the Prussian nobility, and so East Prussia was not only important strategically; it was also a tempting prize for the Russian Army who relished the thought of conquering a place of such symbolic significance.

Hence the Russian Army made its move, snatching Eastern Prussia while the Germans were looking the other way. But the German Kaiser was not to be cheated of the great kingdom for long. Licking his lips at the prospect of regaining Eastern Prussia from Cossack control, he recalled the eminent General Paul von Hindenburg from retirement and put under his command 150,000 men, many of them redirected swiftly from the front line in the west to face this new enemy in the east.

Now, alongside his impressive military knowledge, General von Hindenburg had a second deadly weapon. Prussian-born, he knew the landscape upon which he was about to meet the Russian Army like the back of his hand. It was a waterlogged realm of vast lakes, thick forests, treacherous bogs and sodden marshes, and von Hindenburg knew how to weave a safe path for his men between them, using the kingdom's natural defences to his army's advantage.

So it was that, even though they were outnumbered, the German Army managed to outmanoeuvre the Russians. Like fish caught in deadly nets, isolated pockets of Russian soldiers were trapped in the narrow spaces of passable land between the swamps, while others were driven into bogs where they and their guns were sucked fast into the mud. Some, trying desperately to escape, were forced to attempt to cross the lakes, where they met a hopeless, watery death.

By the end of August 1914, tens of thousands of defeated Russian soldiers were being led away as prisoners and their leader, General Samsonov, was dead. But the battle-hungry Paul von Hindenburg had not finished yet. His tail up, he chased after the remaining retreating Russians, crossing the Russian frontier and clashing with the enemy near Augustovo.

Once again, von Hindenburg was rewarded with a German victory, and his jubilant troops occupied the nearby town of Suwalki.

However, now it was the turn of the esteemed Prussian-German general to be tricked. Too confident, perhaps, in his own abilities, or carried away by his successes, von Hindenburg had advanced too far. While he and his men were caught up in the fighting at Augustovo, additional Russian troops crept up on them from the rear. Led by the General Pavel Rennenkampf, these fresh Russian forces had regrouped behind the Niemen River, and now had the unsuspecting Germans surrounded.

Late at night, on the eve before they made their surprise attack, a well-respected captain in Rennenkampf's slumbering camp was woken by a young soldier. Rushing into the captain's tent, the soldier begged for his superior officer's forgiveness for disturbing him, but stressed that there was something which the captain simply had to see.

The soldier led the captain to the treeline at the edge of the camp and pointed towards the sky.

Looking up, the puzzled captain saw at once a vision which was so instantly recognisable, so miraculous, that he staggered backwards in shock. Indeed, had it not been for the quick reflexes of the soldier and his strong, steadying arm, the captain would have surely fallen to the ground. Entranced, he found himself gazing into the soft, compassionate eyes of the Virgin Mary.

Floating in the inky sky, the Blessed Virgin cradled the infant Christ in her left arm, while her right hand was outstretched, one delicate finger pointing to the west.

Dumbstruck, the captain and the young soldier simply stared at the heavenly apparition, uncertain what to believe but certain that they should not – could not – avert their gaze.

After a few moments, the Virgin Mary vanished, but where her shape had illuminated the sky before them, there was now a shining cross. Instinctively, both soldiers got down onto their knees, overcome with emotion, and they remained there on the ground until the cross, too, faded away and the sky was dark once again.

The captain and the young soldier returned to the camp and to their individual quarters, neither daring to speak to anyone of the vision they had encountered.

As he tossed and turned on his bunk, chasing sleep, the captain contemplated the meaning of the

Virgin Mary's visitation. He was certain that it was a sign of God's blessing, and by dawn he had made the decision to lead his troops boldly to the west.

The very next morning, that same Russian captain rode with his men into the Battle of Augustovo. For nine long days they chased the German Army towards the Masurian Lakes, and although General von Hindenburg's knowledge of the marshes and the woods helped many to escape, 60,000 German soldiers were killed, wounded or taken prisoner.

As the vision of the Virgin had suggested, the Russians were to be victorious.

THE BROTHER WHO RETURNED

If the Tommies felt remote from their families and friends when just the width of the English Channel separated them, one can only wonder how the Australian or Canadian soldiers who came to aid their Commonwealth brothers felt when they were half the world away – or at least the width of the Atlantic Ocean – from their loved ones. Perhaps we shouldn't be surprised that support for them came from the most unlikely quarter … even from beyond the grave, as the following Canadian legend reveals.

In early 1916, Will Bird, a fit young Canadian man, sat in his forest-side home in British Columbia, Canada, shining his best black boots with a mixture of polish and spittle in equal proportions. He was undertaking this task with gusto as he was about to venture into town to the Army Recruiting Centre to join up; something his elder brother, Steve, had done the previous year. Will knew that his brother had been posted to Europe to aid the Allied war effort against the troops of Kaiser Wilhelm and felt that his joining up would only serve to reunite the two of them.

If only he had known!

There was a sharp knock at the back door. Will's mother called him to answer it. Opening the heavy oak door revealed an army officer in full uniform, with plenty of scrambled egg (that is, gold braid) on both cap and lapels.

The officer saluted.

Will called his mother, who immediately burst into tears. This could only be bad news.

The officer gently told Will and his mother that brother and son, Steve, had gone missing in action. Then, after performing all the usual necessities and reassuring Mrs Bird that she should be proud of her son, who had been a much-loved comrade and who had perished for a worthwhile cause, the officer saluted and headed up the road to deliver further tragic news. The Birds would not be the only family in that remote Canadian community mourning a loss that night.

If Mrs Bird's first reaction was to sob for the loss of her eldest son, her second was to try to persuade her younger son, Will, not to go and join up. She hadn't gone to the pain of pregnancy and motherhood, she said, to produce handsome young sons as cannon fodder.

Will considered his mother's words while shedding a tear himself for the passing of his older brother, who had always been a hero and a role model for him. But this same thought process led him to thinking that if the cause had been important enough for Steve to surrender his young life, then perhaps he owed it to Steve's memory to join the campaign.

So, with a tear in his eye but with his head held high and gleaming boots on his feet, Will marched down to the Recruiting Office and joined a regiment soon to be posted to Flanders on the French-Belgian border.

A year later, on 12 April 1917, and by then elevated to the rank of corporal, Will Bird was fighting in the Battle of Vimy Ridge. Lying in an exhausted sleep in a shell hole, Will was squashed together with companions from his platoon under a tarpaulin.

In the middle of the night, Will was shaken from his slumber by two warm and familiar hands. Half asleep, Will was amazed to see standing next to him his brother, Steve.

Despite Will's anxious questions, Steve remained silent, gesturing the younger brother to follow him 100 yards downwind to another shell hole.

As the two brothers lay side by side under a tarpaulin in that shell hole, Will was aware of a slight, strange smell of wet clay about Steve. Too tired to fret, however, he soon fell into an exhausted sleep once again.

At first light, Will woke to discover himself alone, the tarpaulin and his brother both gone. Had they ever been there?

Confused, Will staggered back to the shell hole where he had been with his platoon the night before, and there he discovered a scene almost too terrible to describe. That first hole had taken a direct hit and his comrades lay where Will had left them, their bodies now smashed and lifeless. Only then did Will realise that his brother, or the ghost of his brother, had returned with the sole purpose of saving his life.

Will survived several more tough scrapes and, in 1918, returned to his mother in that little forest-side home in British Columbia, Canada, with a service medal and this remarkable story to tell.

THE HAUNTED HILLS

The Battle of Verdun, which took place from 21 February to 19 December 1916, was one of the costliest confrontations of the First World War. It is said that, by the end of it, more than 360,000 French soldiers and nearly 340,000 German soldiers had lost their lives. The conflict centred on the small French city of Verdun on the River Meuse, which had served as a fortress since Roman times and therefore was a strong symbol of military power. The Germans knew that the French would not want to lose control of it and that they would therefore commit all the manpower they could in order to defend it. This was a chance, the German military leaders believed, to inflict heavy losses upon the French and so clear the way to a subsequent attack on the nation which they considered to be their real enemy: the British.

The following story comes from the middle stages of the Battle of Verdun, during the summer months of May, June and July, when the focus of the German attack was on two hills in particular – Cote (or Hill) 304 and another mound referred to as Le Mort Homme, or The Dead Man.

North-west of the French fortress city of Verdun, there is a small hill known locally as Le Mort Homme, or The Dead Man. The place was so called because, years before the Great War, it was here that the dead body of a stranger was found. No one knew who the man was, where he came from, nor how he had been killed. The mystery was never solved, but from that point on the hill was always referred to by its new name. It was a name that turned out to be a prophetic one too for, in 1916, the hill was the site of one of the bloodiest battles of the First World War, and by the end of the fighting, its slopes were covered with hundreds more corpses – the bodies of dead soldiers.

The Germans had had their eye on Le Mort Homme and the nearby hill, Cote 304, for some time, being aware that these two neighbouring mounds were important lookout points for the

French and could be the key which unlocked the gates into Verdun. Hungry for victory, they launched their attack from both land and air.

Thousands of artillery guns, hundreds of thousands of troops and millions of shells were made ready and the skies were filled with more planes than had been seen at any other battle in history.

Bravely, the French returned fire and men fell on both sides. The days passed, and back and forth went the advantage, each attack followed hot on its heels by a counter-attack. Rain came, falling as heavily as the wounded who, sucked into the oozing mud, were buried alive before they could be rescued.

So long did the battle continue that supplies began to dwindle and fatigue gripped the soldiers who could find no food or fresh water to sustain them. Bound to their trenches, they cried out in thirst and one poor German was so desperate that he threw himself prostrate into a foul-stinking green pond just to feel some moisture on his lips.

Yet, as exhausted as they were, the German battalions' response was not to give up – but to step up – the attack. More men and more ammunition were found and the French felt the force of both, until the hills echoed with the screams and the moans of the wounded and the dying.

The sheer weight of their numbers and their determination to succeed became the German Army's best defence. They did not stop to mourn their comrades when the French gunned them down; instead they used their dead bodies as protection, turning their corpses into macabre shields and, inch by inch, they advanced higher up the hill.

So it was that finally they conquered the two blood-soaked peaks. First to fall was Cote 304, and from their new vantage point the Germans bombarded their enemy, now struggling below them, until the air was thick with choking dust and the planes flying overhead had to swerve for fear of flying blindly into the hillside through clouds of pure black. The earth shook as the barrage of shells blasted into the flanks of Le Mort Homme until that, too, fell into German hands.

But, having fought so hard to take the two hills, the Germans were stopped in their tracks. News came of a Russian attack on the Eastern Front and reinforcements were needed to strengthen the German lines.

Seeing the chance to dwindle German numbers further, the French came up with a cunning plan. They convinced their British friends to bring forward their scheduled offensive on the River Somme, moving it from August to July, knowing the Germans would need to respond.

Their plan worked.

In spite of the hundreds of thousands of men the German Army had lost, and the hundreds of thousands of enemy soldiers they had killed, Verdun was no longer their big prize. They had tried to bleed the French to death but their self-inflicted wounds proved to be just as deep and as great, and at the end of it all, they had made no ground. As December came and the French pushed back, the German lines were back where they were at the start of the battle.

Even today, visitors to the hills of Cote 304 and Le Mort Homme can still see the wounds of this immense and fruitless battle. The landscape is gnarly and pockmarked, scarred for ever from the hailstorms of shells. So much of Cote 304 has been blown into dust that its peak is a whole seven metres lower than it was a century ago. Everywhere you look there are overgrown bunkers, crumbling gun posts, faded trench lines and monuments to the fallen. This is an eerie, evocative, disturbing place and more than once, while taking battlefield tours around Le Mort Homme, visitors have reported hearing the sound of an old aircraft coming over the hill. They look to the sky and see, they say, a German fighter plane flying low over the brow of the hill, trailing fire and smoke. The plane then disappears behind the crest of Cote 304 and the sky falls silent once more.

There are many who have claimed that this is the ghost of the German ace pilot Oswald Boelcke (an 'ace' pilot being one who shot down five or more enemy planes), dubbed the 'Father of the German fighter air force'. Although only twenty-five years old in 1916, Boelcke had already been awarded the highest military honour and there is no doubt that he was in charge of the air attack at Verdun for part of the battle. Yet it was not an enemy pilot who ended Boelcke's life, nor did he die over Verdun. Rather, on 28 October 1916, during a dogfight with British planes over Douai in Northern France, his plane's upper wing was clipped by a friendly aircraft. Not wearing a helmet, and not strapped into his seat properly, Boelcke had no chance of surviving the crash landing. His life was snuffed out in an instant.

Even if it is not the ghost of Boelcke who still haunts the hills near Verdun, if the sightings are to be believed then there is certainly at least one mysterious, unidentified, German First World War pilot who has never given up the fight for those two haunting hills.

Three

Tales of Extraordinary Folk

UNSUNG HEROES

The First World War has left us with some truly memorable tales of great deeds, extraordinary bravery and amazing courage. A small selection of these have been retold on the following pages, but in writing them we were mindful that every man and woman who served his or her country in 1914–18 was, in some way, extraordinary. Every day they were facing tough and challenging conditions, far from home and their loved ones, and yet many of their experiences and personal acts of courage are either long-forgotten or recorded only in personal diaries, postcards and letters home. As a result, we felt it appropriate to preface this chapter with a couple of examples.

The first is an extract from the diary of Edward Victor French (1887–1965). A miller and farmer from Merriott in Somerset, Edward was also Taffy Thomas' grandfather, and fought on the Gallipoli Peninsula in Turkey in 1915.

1915

Went in first line of trenches on the 15th October for 24 hours. On Sunday the 17th, the Turks bombarded us all morning. Major Greg and Pte Blackmore were killed. Went in the trenches on the 19th again.

October 27th: Had a narrow escape. A shrapnel shell burst over me coming back from base. Bullets came all around me.

28th October: The Turks gave us about a dozen shrapnel shells. I was in my dug-out; one bullet came and just touched my foot. Two shells pitched in our dug-out killing and wounding. About 7 p.m. we were relieved by the Notts & Derby.

On the Sunday we had to pack up again and march about 6.5 miles across the salt lake. Then we had to go in the reserve trenches. Our kit bags were taken away so we had to carry all our kit in our packs.

We took over the line of trenches from the Scotch horse on the 18th November at Sedd el Bahr. We stayed there for 5 days then the Devons relieved us and we went back to reserve. We stayed there for 2 days and on the Friday night, the 26th, the rain came down in streams and before we could get out of our dug-out, the water was up to our knees. We had to stay out all night. The trenches were nearly full of water and we lost nearly everything we had. We had to settle in until the Sunday when we went back to some more trenches.

On the Saturday it snowed and then we had a sharp frost. My toes were frost bitten. On the Sunday when we came back to the other trenches it was too cold to sleep so we walked about all night.

Next day we left, relieved by the Welsh. We marched to Lala Baba near the sea. We had bread today, the first for a fortnight.

Helen Watts' great-grandfather, Archibald 'Archie'
Oldham, was born in Rochdale in 1888. He served as a
private in the 1st Manchester Regiment throughout the
Great War and, in March 1918, travelled with his divi-
sion to Egypt and then on to Palestine. While fighting
in Palestine, he was shot in the neck and subsequently
brought home to the UK, to be treated in a military hos-
pital. During his years overseas, he sent many postcards
home, including this one, to his four-year-old daughter
(Helen's grandmother), Sarah.

Dear little girl,

I send this card to you so you will know that your loving
Dad has not forgotten you and never will do. You must be
a good girl, love, for your Mamma and do not give her any
trouble because she is good to you and to me as your Dad.
Try to cheer Mamma up and write me a letter yourself so
that I can show these boys here that you can write.

Good night. God bless. Dad

FROM BATTLEFIELD TO MOVIE SCREEN: THE STORY OF SERGEANT YORK

This is the story of a real First World War hero who became
a Hollywood legend: Alvin C. York, who was immor-
talised in the 1941 Academy Award-winning movie
Sergeant York, *starring Gary Cooper. The brave deed for*
which Alvin became famous took place during the Battle of
the Argonne Forest (26 September–11 November 1918).

This battle was part of the last – and the largest – offensive engagement in which the American Expeditionary Force (AEF) was involved during the Great War.

In reward for his bravery during this crucial turning point in the war, Alvin was awarded an almost unprecedented collection of medals. In his home country of America, he was given the Congressional Medal of Honour, the Distinguished Service Cross, the First and Second World War Victory Medals and the American Campaign Medal. In addition, Montenegro awarded him a War Medal, Italy awarded him the Croce di Guerra al Merito and in France he received the Legion of Honour and the Croix de Guerre.

In the many versions of Sergeant York's story which exist, some details – such as the number of soldiers he led, killed single-handedly or captured – vary. Some people, including the Hollywood movie makers, were keen to capitalise on the story's potential for propaganda, recognising how it could rouse American patriotism as the Second World War drew closer. Therefore, Alvin's heroism and aspects of his life after the war became exaggerated and romanticised. Large helpings of fiction were blended with the facts and, once mixed, it becomes hard for the general public to ever separate the two again. The 1941 movie, for example, ends with Alvin and his girlfriend Gracie running hand in hand into a beautiful new farm which has been built for Alvin by the people of Tennessee. In reality, although the intention was there among the local people to build a new farm for their war hero, the Nashville Rotary failed to raise sufficient funds and defaulted on the instalment payments on the land.

The burden of the remaining debt – and an unfinished farm, lacking in appropriate equipment – was therefore passed on to Alvin.

Meanwhile, other retellings of the story of Sergeant York suggest that he received too much of the credit for his platoon's success and try to promote the part which some of his fellow soldiers played at Argonne, including Sergeant Early and Corporal Cutting – two men who were later awarded the Distinguished Service Cross in 1927.

But whichever version of the story you hear, there seems little doubt that Sergeant York's actions in that French forest in October 1918 deserve to be classified as heroic, and there is no evidence to suggest that he was consciously trying to be a hero. Summing up his actions, York explained: 'I didn't want to go and fight and kill. But I had to answer the call of my country, and I did. And I believed it was right. I have got no hatred toward the Germans and I never had.'

Nor does it appear that York was actively seeking fame on his return to the USA. Writing in his diary on 22 May 1919, during a visit to New York where he carried out a set of interviews with newspaper reporters, he wrote:

It was very nice. But I sure wanted to get back to my people where I belonged, and the little old mother and the little mountain girl who were waiting. And I wanted to be in the mountains again and get out with hounds, and tree a coon or knock over a red fox. And in the midst of the crowds and the dinners and receptions I couldn't help thinking of these things. My thoughts just wouldn't stay hitched.

Alvin York's story is a classic example of the birth of a legend: a man from humble beginnings, never predicted to amount to much, goes off to war and becomes a national hero, and from thereon in his story takes on an extraordinary life of its own.

This is our version of his incredible tale.

Alvin Cullum York was born on 13 December 1887 in Pall Mall, Tennessee. His home was a simple one – a small, two-roomed log cabin in a poor, rural landscape where life was hard and money was scarce. Alvin shared that humble home with ten brothers and sisters, and to place enough food in the pot to feed a family of such size, his father had to juggle the farming of his own patch of land with a part-time job as a blacksmith.

There wasn't much call for reading and writing in a place like Pall Mall back then. It was more important for Alvin to help his father work the land and learn how to hunt. With only nine months of schooling to his name, Alvin devoted his time instead to perfecting his aim with a shotgun, and soon there were very few squirrels, raccoons, deer or wild boar which could dodge the bullets of this precocious young marksman.

Alvin grew into a tall, healthy, strapping young man. Now ready to go out and earn a wage, he secured a day job working on the railroads. Suddenly, he was in the company of men who laboured hard all day and rewarded themselves by playing hard at night. Alvin threw himself headlong into this new world; too fast, perhaps. Rarely had he ever had two spare cents to rub together, yet now he frequently found himself with a day's pay in his hand and no idea of how to spend it wisely. He succumbed to the temptations of drink and gambling, overindulging in both to the point where, far too often, his nights ended with a bar-room brawl.

Soon Alvin had a reputation as bad as his thirst, and the simple folk of Pall Mall wrote him off as yet another troublemaker who would not amount to much.

Ironically, Alvin might have continued heading down that disastrous path into self-destruction were it not for one particularly violent fight which broke out in a bar just over the county line into Kentucky. This time though, it was not Alvin at the centre of it but his best friend, Everett, and the results were tragic. By the time order had been restored and the night was over, Everett was dead.

The death of his best friend hit Alvin hard, and deep in his grief he swore he would change his ways. There would be no more drinking, no more gambling and certainly no more fighting. Rather than looking for trouble, Alvin now looked for God. On the first day of the year 1915, he converted to the Church of Christ in Christian Union and promised to abide by its rules against violence.

As well as faith and a new-found peace of mind, Alvin's religion brought him the chance of love, for it was through his Church that he met his sweetheart – Gracie, the woman who would later become his wife. But, having found one another, the two young lovers were soon to be torn apart, for on 5 June 1917, six months before Alvin was to celebrate his thirtieth birthday, he received a request to register for the draft. The Great War in Europe was calling his name.

The reformed Alvin loved his country and his Church in equal measure, and so he was thrown into turmoil. His conscience led him this way and that, as he tried to ascertain the right path to take. In the end, his determination to leave his violent days behind him won out. Returning his papers to the Draft Board, he requested exemption on the grounds that he simply did not want to fight.

To the American army, Alvin's objection to fighting was little more than an irritating housefly to be batted aside, and his draft papers were sent flying straight back at him. Alvin C. York was, without question, to report immediately for training in the 82nd Infantry Division of the 328th Regiment.

Seeing his rookie soldier's distress, Alvin's commanding officer knew just what to do. A fellow student of the Bible, he directed Alvin to passages in the Holy Book which helped justify violence in times of war. Taking comfort from those words, Alvin accepted his fate while his senior offer accepted that he had in his command a crack-shot marksman with no stomach for war.

The following May, the day finally came for the 82nd Infantry Division to set sail for France.

For Alvin, this was not only the first time he had ever travelled more than fifty miles from his home; it was also the first time he had ever seen the ocean and he was overcome by the vast expanse of water surrounding him. Seasickness gripped him so hard that even the thought of the battlefields which lay waiting across the water did not quell his desire to be back on dry land.

And perhaps it was during this, his first battle of the war on an unfamiliar journey across the sea, against a wild and unpredictable enemy, that Alvin formed an unbreakable bond with the fellow men in his platoon. Certainly, by the time he stepped ashore in France, he was ready to fight to the death alongside them.

By October 1918, Alvin and his division were fighting their way through what was left of the woods of the Argonne Forest. Burned and broken by the shelling, the trees around them formed a frightening, grotesque silhouette against the fiery skies, and the ground underfoot was pockmarked and treacherous. As they headed for the front line, Alvin and his companions had to scramble over the corpses of slaughtered men and horses, while shells burst in their ears and enemy planes buzzed over their heads.

Desperate to halt the German bombardment, their platoon commander came up with a plan. He knew that the key was gaining control of the Decauville railroad behind a hill known as Hill 223. Swiftly, he ordered Alvin and sixteen other infantrymen to sneak behind the enemy lines and secure the German machine-gun post at the top of the hill, taking it by surprise from the rear.

Swallowing their fear, the men began to make their way quietly up the hill, staying low and out of sight in the brush. Undetected, they advanced a good 300 yards in front of their own line and took several prisoners before the alarm was raised.

When the counter-attack came, it was deadly.

Turning their machine guns around and thinking that they were about to be overwhelmed by a wave of American troops, the Germans opened fire in unison, throwing everything they had at their attackers.

Their targets were now so close they were hard to miss. Bullets ripped the lifeblood from six of them, and three more fell down wounded. With more than half of his tiny squad mown down, including his sergeant, Alvin took command. Thinking on his feet, his hunting instincts, drilled into him from when he was just a boy back in Tennessee, kicked in.

Alvin ordered everyone to stay down low, to take cover in the brush and to guard the prisoners. Then he began a single-handed move which not one of his enemy – nor perhaps, his countrymen – could ever have predicted.

As the machine-gun fire whistled over the heads of his crouching platoon, Alvin alone stood his ground, held his breath and took aim. He remembered how his father had taught him to shoot wild turkeys back home on the farm in Pall Mall: one by one, taking out the one closest to the back of the flock first, then the second, then third and on and on, so no single creature was aware that the ones behind him had fallen, until every last target was struck.

Seventeen German gunners were picked off by Alvin's keen sniper's eye. Then six more leapt out of their trench in fury, charging at the solo American assassin with their bayonets. Finding courage he never knew he had, Alvin did not move as he emptied his rifle of bullets and switched calmly to his pistol. In a matter of seconds, there were six more Germans dispatched to their graves.

The major in command of the German gun posts made his move, but nothing and no one was going to stop Alvin now. He was on top of the major in an instant and, before the German could issue a cry for help, Alvin had a gun to his head. With their major's life hanging in the balance, the remaining Germans on the hill rushed to surrender. And so it was that just eleven American soldiers – and three of them wounded – led 132 German prisoners back down the hill and made it to safety alongside the rest of their division behind the front line.

So incredible was Alvin's achievement, so stunning was his bravery, that he was made a sergeant and given the highest military honour in America – the Congressional Medal of Honour. But it was not fame and fortune which Alvin longed for on his return, nor did he court the hero's welcome which he received. Rather it was a safe return to his beloved home in the mountains, and the beautiful woman who awaited him there, that formed his true prize.

So years later, when Hollywood wanted his permission to tell his story on the silver screen, Alvin took some convincing.

'This uniform ain't for sale!' he cried, and went back to his jobs on the farm.

But the movie makers would not give up and they had one more trick up their sleeve. What if Alvin's favourite film star, Gary Cooper, were to agree to play his part?

Alvin was swayed and, promising to use his royalties to build a new Bible school, he signed the contract. The movie went on to win its handsome leading actor an Academy Award and Alvin became a war legend all over the world.

As promised, he did not allow his fame to bring him fortune, and when he died at the age of seventy-six on 2 September 1964, Alvin was back where he started in life, with barely two spare cents to rub together. But America would never forget its hero: it would never forget the day that Sergeant Alvin C. York went beyond the call of duty in the forests of Argonne in 1918. He was buried in the cemetery in his home town of Pall Mall, with full military honours and a State Governor and an official representative of President Lyndon B. Johnson among the chief mourners.

LEGEND OF THE SKIES

The Story of Gilbert Insall

Gilbert Stuart Martin Insall (14 May 1894–17 February 1972) was born and educated in Paris. Having first joined the army through the University and Public Schools Brigade of the Royal Fusiliers, he then became a second lieutenant in 11 Squadron of the British Royal Flying Corps at the age of twenty-one. After just four months in that post, he was sent to the Western Front. Later that year, on 7 November 1915, he did something so courageous that it earned him the highest award for gallantry in war – the Victoria Cross. The following tale of Insall's brave actions is adapted from an account written in March 1918 by Captain James Price Lloyd of the Welsh Regiment, who served with the British Military Intelligence unit known as MI7. Central to the role of this department was censorship and propaganda, so it is no surprise that Captain Lloyd was given the task of recording the kind of events which led war heroes like Insall to be awarded the Victoria Cross.

We are fortunate to have this account today. The type-script was among those propaganda archives which MI7 destroyed after the war in an attempt to prevent sensitive information from reaching the general public. However, Captain Lloyd kept his own handwritten version of the story.

Gilbert Insall was one of the few lucky ones who saw and survived two world wars. He died in England on 17 February 1972, at the age of seventy-seven. His headstone can be seen in the graveyard at All Saints church in the village of Nocton in Lincolnshire, while his Victoria Cross is on display at the Royal Air Force Museum at Hendon.

This is the true story of how two British airmen and two German pilots fought a duel in the skies over Northern France, and what became of them.

On the afternoon of 9 November 1915, Second Lieutenant Gilbert Insall and his gunner, 1st Class Air Mechanic Thomas Donald, were on patrol in their Vickers biplane over the town of Achiet, south of Arras. At about 2.30 p.m., Donald, keeping a lookout from his cramped cockpit at the front of the plane, spotted a two-man, enemy Aviatik craft some 1,000 feet above, heading south. He shouted to his pilot, who at once lifted the Vickers' nose and began to climb steadily after the German plane.

Whether or not the German pilot and his companion were immediately aware of the danger of attack, we cannot be sure, but either way they appeared to have other business to attend to that day, for they carried on their way south, without diverting from their course. Having the faster plane, the German pilot was soon putting more and more distance between himself and his two British pursuers.

Seeing that the German plane was too remote a target for his machine gun, Donald reached for his rifle in the hope that a lucky shot might reach its mark. Once, twice, three times he fired, each time missing his target but succeeding in both alerting and annoying the enemy pilot. When the German responded by turning and speeding back towards the British plane, Insall banked and flew westwards towards Achiet. The German followed, the hunted now the hunter.

Just as they flew over the town, Insall suddenly turned again, sharply this time, catching his adversary by surprise.

Before the German pilot had a chance to respond, bullets were whistling by his head. But he still had one more card to play. Just a few minutes' flight to the north, near the village of Heninel, lay a certain rocket battery, whose job it was to shoot down any British aircraft which dared to come their way. The German knew that if he could lead the British airman into this deadly trap, he would be safe.

He sped northwards, drawing Insall closer and closer towards the battery. Then, just before he reached it, he turned, hoping that the Vickers would not have time to react and would fly blindly into a hail of enemy fire. But he was too late. As he banked, he was caught in Donald's firing line.

Strafed with bullets, the engine of the Aviatik spluttered and cut out. For a moment everything was silent, then, with smoke streamers trailing, the plane began to spin, over and over, dropping from the sky like an autumn leaf. However, to the amazement of Insall and Donald who were watching intensely from above, the German pilot managed to control the spin and brought his aircraft into a steep glide towards the earth, 6,000 feet below.

With the roar of the Vickers in his ears and bullets grazing his wings, the German airman knew that this time he did not have the luxury of choosing his landing site. But drawing on all the lessons he had learned during his hours of flying, he managed to land safely, although heavily, in a ploughed field.

In panic, the pilot and his companion scrambled out of the damaged plane, taking their machine gun with them, and made off across the muddy furrows. Then, as they heard the Vickers descending rapidly behind them, they halted, turned their gun on the British airmen and opened fire.

Insall had had enough. Flying as low as he dared, he swooped down like an eagle about to snatch its prey and screamed at Donald to cut the pair down. Donald let rip with his gun and the two Germans were sprayed with soil as bullets tore into the ground around them. Dropping their machine gun, they fled for their lives into the shelter of a clump of trees on the far side of the field, one of them taking a wounding bullet before he disappeared into the greenery.

With the airmen chased like scared rabbits into the undergrowth, Insall brought the Vickers about again. He descended to 300 feet and slowed sufficiently to enable Donald to drop an incendiary bomb on the crashed Aviatik, transforming it into a blazing inferno.

However, 300 feet is not a healthy height at which to be flying over enemy lines, and Insall knew that he had to gain altitude again as quickly as he could and head for safety. But they were not out of danger yet. Their return route meant running the gauntlet; flying over lines of enemy trenches.

Recognising the markings of a British craft, the Germans below opened fire without a moment's hesitation. Shells exploded above and below the little plane and bullets whistled between the struts of the wings. The Vickers rocked dangerously but Insall kept her steady, while Donald returned fire at the enemy below, emptying three drums.

On they flew, crossing right over the German line. Then, just when safety seemed assured, the engine stopped. The Vickers been hit. There was nothing for it but to glide down, hoping for as safe a landing as the Aviatik had enjoyed just minutes before.

Matching the German pilot's skill, Insall made an emergency landing near a small wood just 500 yards inside the Allied lines, but the plane had barely touched the ground before the first German shell came screaming through the air. Anxious to save their precious plane and maintain a means by which to continue their voyage home, Insall and Donald dragged the craft into the trees, just managing to keep it out of reach of the falling shells which rained down on them for the rest of the afternoon. More than 150 shells landed on the edge of that wood, but thankfully not one of them made a direct hit.

After radioing their nearest aerodrome to send the parts they needed, the two British men waited bravely for darkness to fall. When it finally did so and the breakdown party arrived, Insall and his mechanic set to work on the plane, fixing it quietly by torchlight.

As soon as dawn came, the gallant pair took to the air once more and, after a final swoop along the German trenches, turned for home.

For his share in this adventurous enterprise, Second Lieutenant Gilbert Insall was awarded the Victoria Cross, while his companion, 1st Class Air Mechanic Thomas Donald, was awarded the Distinguished Conduct Medal.

But, before he collected his award from the king at Buckingham Palace, Insall had further wartime adventures to face. Barely a month after his exploits at Achiet, he found himself once again chasing an enemy aircraft behind German lines. But this time he was not so lucky. He did not come out unscathed. A shell which exploded below his biplane sent fragments slicing through the floor and into Insall's spine. Nonetheless, even while drifting in and out of consciousness, he managed to land the plane safely, only to be captured by German soldiers on the ground.

Insall was operated on while in a prisoner-of-war camp, and as soon as he was back on his feet was causing trouble for the enemy once again, escaping twice over the next two years. Finally, on a third attempt, he made it to freedom, travelling on foot with two fellow escapees into Holland. The ordeal took them nine long and dangerous nights.

Seeing active service in one war, and earning a Victoria Cross, might have been enough for most men. But the amazing Gilbert Insall not only survived the Great War; he also went on to serve in 51 Squadron in the Second World War.

Even when he was not in military action in the air, Insall still made his mark as a pilot, for it was he who, while flying near to Stonehenge one day in 1925, first noticed an unusual arrangement of pits in the ground below. Insall recorded what he saw in photographs that were later used by archaeologists to identify the Bronze Age site of Woodhenge.

Gilbert Insall – the man who had become a legend in his own right, had discovered a land of legends dating as far back as 2300 BC.

THE STORY OF EDITH CAVELL

We should not be surprised how many stories and legends have their roots in the First World War. Those tumultuous years of 1914–18 created thousands of heroes – people from all walks of life who showed amazing bravery, tenacity and selflessness when it mattered most. Stories about them were often shared among those fighting on the battlefield; some travelled home to families and friends, written in letters and diaries or immortalised in lines of poetry or prose; a few were passed down through generations and have found their place in legend.

Millions of war heroes never made it into the pages of our storybooks, and they lie quietly in unmarked graves, their stories long forgotten, but one person whose story did secure a place in legend is British nurse, Edith Cavell (4 December 1865– 12 October 1915). Edith did not become famous until after her death and, although undeniably deserving of her legendary status, it is possible that her story would have been buried hurriedly along with her body, had the British Government not chosen to champion her as a war hero.

This is Edith's life story.

Edith Cavell was born on 4 December 1865 in the small Norfolk village of Swardeston. Her father, Frederick, was the vicar of the village church, and her mother, Louisa Sophia, was the daughter of Frederick's housekeeper.

Edith's first home was a temporary one, for not long after she was born, she and her parents moved into a brand new vicarage next to the church. This was no lavish statement, no needless spending of Church funds, for the money for the building of the vicarage came from Edith's father's own pocket.

Frederick's desire to leave a legacy for his community took all of his family's savings. But even so, Frederick continued to display generosity towards his parishioners, demonstrating to them and his family that charity really did start at home: Frederick and Louisa Sophia were even known to share out their Sunday roast with their neighbours.

More Cavell children soon followed, in the form of Florence, then Lilian and finally little John, whom they all called Jack. The Cavells were a close family and Edith benefitted from a caring and loving start to her life. Within this nurturing environment, she grew into a confident and enterprising young teenager. No teenage rebellion for her; rather she channelled her energies into positive things. One day, while helping her mother in the Sunday school, Edith noticed how cramped the children were. So that very same afternoon, she wrote to the Bishop of Norwich, asking his approval for a new Sunday schoolroom.

With permission granted, Edith promptly set up a fundraising campaign, selling greetings cards which she painted herself. In no time at all, the new schoolroom was in place and Edith and her mother could be found there every Sunday, teaching the village children in brand new, more spacious surroundings.

But like a young bird, which inevitably grows too big for its nest, the time came for Edith to leave home and start to find her own way in life. At the sweet age of sixteen, she waved goodbye to her mother and father, and to Florence, Lilian and Jack, and headed off to boarding school.

Edith missed her home, but she was hungry to learn and she showed herself to have a natural talent for speaking French. She longed to be teacher, so as soon as she had passed all her exams, she found a job as a governess.

Edith enjoyed her new role, but was keen to learn more about the world, to expand her knowledge and become the best teacher she could be. So when the generosity of a kind, departed soul saw Edith inherit a modest sum of money, she leapt at the opportunity for her first taste of travel and exploration. She headed for the snow-capped mountains and the lush green valleys of Austria and Bavaria, soaking up the language and culture like a sponge.

It was while on her travels that Edith first came upon a venture which was to change the course of her life. She visited a hospital whose doors were open to everyone, rich or poor, no matter what their background or status, and where all treatment was free. It was run by a man with the memorable name of Doctor Wolfenberg. So impressed was Edith with his charitable approach to medicine that not only did she decide to donate her remaining inheritance to the hospital; she also made up her mind that she was going to become a nurse.

But with no more money to spend, Edith knew she must first return to work as a governess. For the next five years, she cared for the children of a French-speaking Belgian family in the beautiful city of Brussels, using the opportunity to perfect her French.

Although now a mature woman, approaching thirty years of age, Edith still missed her home back in Norfolk and, whenever she had time off, would return to the peace and tranquility of Swardeston and the beautiful vicarage with its moat. And it was during these happy days back home that Edith fell in love with her second cousin, Eddie.

If Edith thought she had found her perfect soulmate, her heart was about to be broken, for on broaching the subject of marriage, she discovered that Eddie had different ideas about their future together. Making excuses about his poor health and his unsuitability as a husband, Eddie instantly retreated to the role of cousin and friend.

However, there was little time for Edith to dwell on her cousin's rejection, for soon all her emotions and her attention were on her father's ailing health. Terrified of losing him, Edith swapped her post in Brussels for a chair by her father's bedside and devoted her time to nursing him back to health. The joy of seeing her father getting better and better each day convinced Edith that nursing was really where her future lay, and as soon as her father was strong enough, she headed for London and signed up at nursing school.

Once again, Edith threw herself into her studies, learned fast and worked hard. She was not afraid of a challenge, no matter how big or small, even risking her own life to help the victims of a typhoid fever outbreak which was threatening to devastate the seaside town of Margate in Kent.

So fine a nurse did Edith show herself to be that she was soon back in Brussels, passing on her skills in a new nurses' training school. But life for Edith – and for the people of Belgium – was about to change again, and for the worse.

Edith's beloved father, Frederick, fell ill once more, and this time lost his battle for life. Then, in August 1914, while she was in Norfolk comforting her widowed mother, Edith heard the shocking news that Germany, under orders from its power-hungry Kaiser, had invaded Belgium.

The grief-stricken Louisa begged her daughter to stay in the relative safety of Britain but Edith, whose sense of duty was strong, knew that the teaching hospital now needed her more than ever, and she hurried back across the sea to Belgium.

If the German Army had expected an easy passage through Belgium to France, it had a nasty surprise, for the people of Belgium, outraged at the invasion, put up a serious fight. Snipers laid in wait for the invaders to arrive, civilians poured into the streets when they did, and the fighting was bloody and merciless. The German soldiers' response was even more ferocious and, in a desperate attempt to maintain control, they swore to take ten Belgian lives for every German soldier lost.

The wounded and the dying poured into Edith's hospital which had now become a Red Cross station and, remembering the neutral approach of her mentor, Doctor Wolfenberg, she refused to turn anyone away. Man, woman or child, patients on both sides of the conflict lay next to one another and benefitted from her care.

Despite the Belgians' best efforts, Brussels fell after only a few days of fighting, and one after the other, Edith's nurses returned to England. With all the German and Dutch nurses sent home, only Edith and one faithful assistant remained, determined to care for the wounded and the sick, whatever their allegiance.

Aware of the dangerous situation she was placing herself in, Edith put pen to paper and scribed a letter to send home to England. 'My darling mother and family,' she wrote:

> If you open this, it will be because that which we fear has now happened, and Brussels has fallen into the hands of the enemy. They are very near now and it is doubtful if the Allied armies can stop them. We are prepared for the worse. I shall think of you to the last, and you may be sure we shall do our duty here and die as women of our race should die. God bless you and keep you safe.

Edith's safety was further put into jeopardy when, one night that autumn, two dishevelled British soldiers turned up at the clinic. On the point of exhaustion, the men told Edith how they had become separated from their battalion in the retreat from Mons. Lost and hungry, they were now stranded in enemy territory, desperately trying to make their way home.

Taking pity on her poor countrymen, Edith gave the men food and water and hid them in her quarters. For the next fourteen days, they remained there in secrecy, recovering from their ordeal, while Edith sought help.

It did not take her long. Soon there was an underground network of forgers, safe houses and guides, ready to furnish the two soldiers with the money, identity papers and maps they needed to make an escape. With the help of this secret team, the soldiers headed north out of Belgium, escaping across the flat fields, canals and dykes of Holland, to the coast.

The two lucky survivors from Mons became the first of more than 200 Allied soldiers who were provided with a safe passage home thanks to Edith's courage and tenacity. One by one, she would nurse them back to health and keep them out of the German prison camps, before engineering their escape.

Edith told no one of her secret activities. She sewed all incriminating paperwork safely inside a cushion in her room and always held her nerve, even when the Germans suspected that she was up to something and carried out a search of the clinic. While Edith calmly showed the soldiers around, her latest charge – a Belgian collaborator – crept out of the back garden unseen.

But Edith's luck was running out, for on 31 July 1915, the German soldiers came back to search the clinic again and this time, when they left, they took Edith with them, her hands bound. Whether they had been tipped off, or whether they had seen Edith acting suspiciously, they did not say. All her captors did tell her was that she was not alone: two others involved in her scheme had also been taken prisoner and they, the captors lied, had confessed all. Poor Edith, who believed what she was being told, admitted defeat and admitted her part.

It took just ten weeks for the Germans to bring Edith to trial and while pleas for her release came from as far away as America and Spain, the British Government remained silent, fearing their intervention would anger the Germans and do Edith more harm than good.

All alone in the dock, Edith's only defence for aiding the Allied soldiers was that had she not helped them, they would have been shot. To her German accusers, this was no defence at all, and Edith was sentenced to be executed the very next day.

The last friendly person that Edith saw before she faced the firing squad came to her that night in the form of an English chaplain. Finding her calm, free of bitterness and resigned to her fate, the chaplain took communion with Edith then they quietly sang 'Abide With Me'. Holding back the tears, Edith gave the chaplain a prayer book, asking that he honour her last wish that it be taken to her cousin back in Swardeston. Only after he left the room did the chaplain glance inside and see that Edith had dedicated the book to her one and only sweetheart, sending her darling Eddie her love.

Edith Cavell and her two fellow conspirators were executed not long after dawn on 12 October 1915. There are those who say that the men in the firing squad could not bear to shoot such a kind and gentle soul, and fired wide. There are those who say that before the guns fired, Edith fainted and was put to death instead by a single pistol shot, fired by a German officer. Others say that one of the gunmen threw down his rifle in protest and was himself shot, alongside Edith, for his disobedience. There is, of course, also the possibility that nothing out of the ordinary happened at all. But whatever the details of Edith's final moments, her body was hurriedly buried close to the firing range and her grave marked with a simple wooden cross.

Edith's life may have been cut short, but the effects of it lived on, as news of her death sent ripples of anger around the world. In trying to make an example of the brave nurse, the Germans had given their enemies all the ammunition they needed for a powerful propaganda campaign. In this shocking story, the Germans were the evil villains and Edith was the perfect patriotic heroine – a symbol of bravery and courage.

So important was Edith's legacy considered to be, that when the war was finally over, special arrangements were made to return her body to Britain where she could be laid to rest back in her beloved church in Swardeston. To mark her life, a memorial was held in her honour at Westminster Abbey, with Queen Alexandra and Princess Victoria in the congregation alongside nurses from all over the world. And in the true spirit of Edith's sense of charity, the Cavell Nurses' Trust was set up in her name, to provide rest homes for retired nurses.

Edith never wanted fame and she never set out to become a martyr. But through her actions, her kindness, her bravery and her courage, she nonetheless became a true legend of the First World War.

WHAT GOES AROUND COMES AROUND

The bones of this story were given to us by Australian storyteller and Bush poet, Ken Prato. Ken – who spent forty-five years of his life working as a sheep-shearer all over Australia – shared the tale while visiting the English seaside town of Whitby to take part in a special event at the Whitby Folk Festival called Taffy's Tunes and Tales. Ken is among the many hundreds of Australian tourists who have visited the French town of Villers-Bretonneux over the years, inspired by the story which here follows of a surprising and long-lasting friendship between two communities on opposite sides of the globe.

Not far from the River Somme in Northern France is a small town called Villers-Bretonneux. Its size belies its significance, for in the spring of 1918, this was the site of the first head-to-head tank battle the world had ever seen.

It was the final year of the Great War, and Germany was executing its last major offensive. As the German troops advanced towards Amiens, Villers-Bretonneux stood in their path. But this was no tiny ant about to be crushed easily underfoot. To win the town, the German forces had to push through British defences. In a clash of the Titans, the Germans pitted their three A7V tanks against three British Mk IV machines, and came out on top. By the end of the day on 24 April 1918, Villers-Bretonneux was occupied and around 3,500 dismayed residents were forced from their homes.

But the people of Villers-Bretonneux were not to be exiled for long: the Australians were coming. After darkness fell that very same day, troops from the 4th and 5th Divisions of the Australian Imperial Forces – known as the AIF – launched a counter-attack.

German flares lit up the skies, turning night into day and casting the Australian soldiers into deadly pools of light amid which they could be picked off, one by one, with machine-gun fire. But the brave soldiers from Down Under kept on coming, wave upon wave, and by morning the tide had turned and they were chasing an enemy ten times their own size back out of the town.

Yet, being so heavily outnumbered meant that victory came at a high price. The AIF were left with 1,200 of their brothers' bodies to bury, more than 10,000 miles away from home, in French soil.

Having fought so hard to regain Villers-Bretonneux, the AIF soldiers were determined that no German would ever set foot in the town again. They stationed a garrison there, amid the war-ravaged buildings, and were welcomed by the locals who were overjoyed at being able to return to their homes – no matter how tattered and torn they were.

As a demonstration of their gratitude, the people of Villers-Bretonneux changed the names of many places in their town. The main street became Rue de Melbourne, a restaurant was fondly renamed Le Kangourou, and one district was newly christened Robinvale, after the town in north-east Victoria from which one group of AIF soldiers came.

Throughout the final months of the war, the AIF remained in Villers-Bretonneux, manning the garrison, and a strong bond of friendship was forged between the French inhabitants and their colonial saviours.

Finally, at war's end, the soldiers said their goodbyes and returned home to Australia, leaving their new French companions to rebuild both their town and their lives. Reunited with their families, the soldiers spoke with affection of the now devastated town that was Villers-Bretonneux and the friendships they had forged. As one by one their stories were shared, a feeling began to emerge ... a determination not to forget but to continue to help their friends working so hard to restore their beloved town, thousands of miles away back in France.

So it was that the people of Victoria decided to raise funds to help rebuild the town's primary school. Schoolchildren all over the state joined in by holding penny-drives, and day by day, week by week, the funds grew until they had raised some £10,000. The sum was matched by the Victoria State Government, and the organisers proudly despatched to France enough money to rebuild the school.

On 25 April 1927 (which, coincidentally, was also Anzac Day), and nine years to the day after the AIF had driven the German invaders out of Villers-Bretonneux, a brand new, two-storey school building was inaugurated in the town. Overwhelmed by the generosity of their Australian friends, the local people named it L'Ecole Victoria, and above every blackboard they installed a sign conveying the message: 'N'oublions jamais l'Australie' or 'Let us never forget Australia'.

Then, on the front of the building, they put up a plaque with the inscription:

This building is the gift of the schoolchildren of Victoria, Australia, to the children of Villers-Bretonneux as a proof of their love and good-will towards France. Twelve hundred Australian soldiers, the fathers and brothers of these children, gave their lives in the heroic recapture of this town from the invader on 24th April 1918, and are buried near this spot. May the memory of great sacrifices in a common cause keep France and Australia together for ever in bonds of friendship and mutual esteem.

If someone ignorant of the story of Villers-Bretonneux passed by the windows of L'Ecole Victoria on the first day of any term-time week – even today – they might hear the children inside singing a surprising song … a song which might seem out of place in rural France. For they would probably hear the words of 'Waltzing Matilda', and they would be witnessing yet another way in which the people of the town remember the generosity of their wartime friends on the other side of the world.

Thousands of Australians who do know the town's history visit Villers-Bretonneux each year to relive the adventures of their forebears and to pay their respects to the dead, lying in one of the beautifully maintained cemeteries on the edge of the town. Most will also visit the Musee Franco-Australien – the museum which was installed in 1975 on the upper floors of the school to house memorabilia representing their country's involvement on the Western Front throughout the First World War – among the artefacts being letters, flags, uniforms, photographs and even a kangaroo mascot.

Our story could finish here. But there is a saying – appropriately with an Australian flavour – which claims that 'kindness, like a boomerang, always returns', and that saying invites one final chapter to the tale …

In the summer of 2009, a series of devastating bush-fires ravaged the state of Victoria and many homes and three schools were destroyed in the blaze. Here was an opportunity for the people of Villers-Bretonneux to repay the kindness shown to them some nine decades earlier. A sum of $21,000 was raised by the French community, and was sent to help fund the rebuilding program.

Some months later, a group from the little French town – including the mayor and thirty citizens – travelled all the way to Australia to be part of the opening ceremony for the new primary school at Strathewen, in central Victoria. And in the courtyard they witnessed the erection of a special plaque, reminiscent of its French counterpart on a similar school 10,000 miles away, which read: 'N'oublions jamais nos amis de Villers-Bretwonneux, France' or 'Never forget our friends in Villers-Bretonneux, France'.

———

The date of 25 April officially became known as Anzac Day in 1916 – one year after the Australian and New Zealand Army Corps landed at Gallipoli in 1915, and took part in their first military action of the Great War. It became a national day of remembrance in Australia in the 1920s and after 1927 it also became a public holiday.

Four

*Humour from
a Dark Place*

THE PHOTO OF THE GIRL I LEFT BEHIND ME

In the period leading up to the Great War, during it and indeed following it, the main forms of entertainment in England were the music halls and variety theatres. Famous artists used their voices for the war effort. Miss Florrie Forde amused audiences with 'It's A Long Way to Tipperary', and 'Take Me Back to Dear Old Blighty'. These were common entertainments for common people, though humour was a touch coarse, and unfettered by any of the sensibilities we have come to know in the twenty-first century with regards to issues of feminism and racism. This was probably not because folk were rude or insensitive, but rather because they were preoccupied with more immediate issues of mortality and survival.

The text of the song that follows, originally from the comic singer Billy Merson (and which Taffy Thomas has heard sung on several occasions by Essex folk singer Simon Ritchie), has to be considered in the context of the 1900s, where it elicited hearty chuckles and belly laughs from both men and women, together enjoying a bit of escape from the death and destruction of Flanders Fields. If you find yourself chuckling likewise, just enjoy those few moments of freedom and guilty pleasure.

The Photo of the Girl I Left Behind Me

When first I made me mind up that a soldier I would be,
The girl that I was courting she came round and said to me
'I've had me photo taken, Bill, and if we are to part
Promise me you'll always wear the photo next your heart.'
She hung the locket round my neck and her ruby lips I kissed
Borrowed the fare to Aldershot and off I went to enlist.

Chorus:
With the photo of the girl I left behind me
I went and joined the army full of glee
Then someone came up to remind me
The doctor wanted to examine me.
When the doctor found the locket next my heart
he said to me
'Whose photograph is this sir that I find?
Is this the captain's bulldog?' I said,
'No, sir, if you please, sir
It's the photo of the girl I left behind.'

I never shall forget the first day that I went under fire
I'd been looking at the photo of the girl that I admire
I thought her lovely face would encourage me to go
And fight like Englishmen should do
when going to face the foe.
The Captain said, 'We're cornered, boys,
so fight like mad you must.'
I kissed the photograph and then
you couldn't see me for dust.

Chorus:
With the photo of the girl I left behind me
I rushed into the thickest of the fray
When the Captain said, 'We're out of ammunition
I'm afraid it's going to be a losing day.'
I said, 'Don't worry over ammunition, if you please
I have something far more terrible you will find
I will rush amongst the enemy and
I'll frighten them to death
With the photo of the girl I left behind.

With the photo of the girl I left behind me
I went to practise shooting one Summer day
When we found a gust of wind had been unkind and
Blown the blooming target right away.
The Captain said, 'The target's gone whatever shall we do?'
I shouted just to cheer him, 'Never mind
If you haven't got a target and
you want something to shoot at
Here's the photo of the girl I left behind.'

Song lyrics written and composed by
Billy Merson (1881–1947)

Billy Merson's song is actually a cheeky version of the following, traditional folk song dating back to the late eighteenth and early nineteenth century, known simply as 'The Girl I Left Behind Me'. The sad words of this traditional song were particularly relevant to the men who went off to the Great War, who would sing it about their loved ones back home.

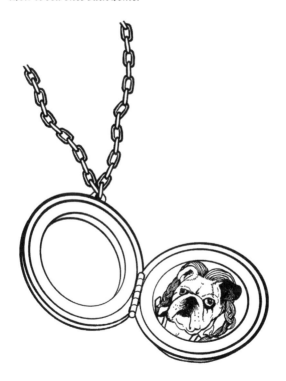

The Girl I Left Behind Me

The hours sad I left a maid
A lingering farewell taking
Whose sighs and tears my steps delayed
I thought her heart was breaking.
In hurried words her name I blest
I breathed the vows that bind me
And to my heart in anguish pressed
The girl I left behind me.

Then to the East we bore away
To win a name in story
And there where dawns the sun of day
There dawned our sun of glory.
The place in my sight
When in the host assigned me
I shared the glory of that fight
Sweet girl I left behind me.

Though many a name our banner bore
Of former deeds of daring
But they were of the day of yore
In which we had no sharing.
But now our laurels freshly won
With the old one shall entwine me
Singing worthy of our size each son
Sweet girl I left behind me.

The hope of final victory
Within my bosom burning
Is mingling with sweet thoughts of thee
And of my fond returning.
But should I n'eer return again
Still with thy love I'll bind me
Dishonors breath shall never stain
The name I leave behind me.

UNDERGROUND MUTTON

An old soldier from the Devonshire Regiment, Wrey Tucker, lived in the small Devon village of South Zeal near Okehampton until his death in 2012. A caretaker at the local primary school, Wrey told the story that follows to Taffy Thomas over several games of cribbage. It's amazing how expensive collecting a new tale can be at a penny a point! Wrey told this as a Second World War story, although conversations indicated it was a First World War story that he had recycled.

The soldiers of the Devonshire Regiment had completed their training on Dartmoor prior to their posting to France, and they had one more training week at the barracks at Catterick Camp in North Yorkshire to endure.

After a long journey, the Devon men settled into their Nissen huts at the barracks, and went down to the mess for a meal. The food was disgusting. The Dartmoor and Exmoor boys all agreed that they had to do something about it.

They noticed that at the back of the officer's mess stood a tatty old upright piano. The visitors stripped some of the strings from the scrapped musical instrument and fashioned some snares. Then they slipped out of camp to the moorland, returning later with about a dozen snared rabbits.

The Devon boys, poachers to a man, knew well what to do next. Using the long nail on each rabbit's foot, they paunched and skinned the dead coneys then they delivered the fresh meat to the kitchen and a fine stew was cooked up.

Sitting down to supper that night was a much more pleasurable experience for both the West Country visitors and their Yorkshire hosts. The colonel of the 'Yorkies' commented on the 'fine tucker', and enquired as to its provenance. One of the Devon boys told him he wouldn't normally disclose such information. However, as they were all in 'that damned war together', he would. He told the Yorkshire officer that, where his boys came from, people called it 'underground mutton'.

Fascinated, the colonel asked how one could acquire such 'underground mutton'.

Mischievously, the Dartmoor private told him that he had to get a bloody great stick and make his way out onto the moors until he spotted a hole in the bank. Then he had to stand by the hole, raise the stick, and make a noise like a carrot. When the brown hairy ears appeared … 'BANG!'

Despite the cheek of the junior soldier, even the dour Yorkshire officer managed a smile, for now even he had a story to tell.

THE CHEF WHO SAVED THOUSANDS OF LIVES

As in the 'underground mutton' story, soldiers on the battlefront during the Great War would sometimes supplement their rations with wild rabbit or – if they were lucky – produce from nearby farms. But undoubtedly, life on the front line was tough and energy-sapping and so it was essential that soldiers were kept well fed – not only to maintain their health but also their morale. Conditions in the trenches were often unsanitary and cooking and storing food in these conditions was never going to be easy. However, thanks to a French chef named Alexis Benoit Soyer (1810–58), cooks were able to provide the troops with adequate meals, cooked well.

Soyer's contribution was an invention he designed in 1849 and which was known as Soyer's Magic Stove. The stove was small enough to be taken anywhere and was powered by pressurised fuel which could become hot enough to cook food – and more importantly to kill any bacteria in the ingredients – in just a few minutes.

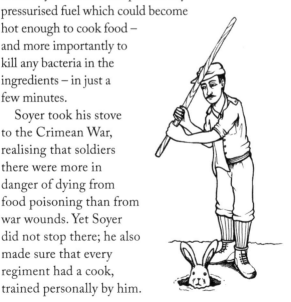

Soyer took his stove to the Crimean War, realising that soldiers there were more in danger of dying from food poisoning than from war wounds. Yet Soyer did not stop there; he also made sure that every regiment had a cook, trained personally by him.

Soyer's Magic Stove was so successful that it travelled with many Victorian explorers on their expeditions and was even used to prepare a meal on the top of one of Egypt's pyramids. Sixty-five years after its invention, the Soyer Stove was also an essential piece of life-saving equipment in the field kitchens of the First World War.

GOOD NEWS AND BAD NEWS

The heavy and light engineering communities around the edge of Birmingham, including places such as Dudley, Walsall, Wolverhampton, Quarry Bank and Cradley Heath, have been known as 'The Black Country' since the Industrial Revolution. The area was famous for chain and nail making; amongst other things. The anchor chain for the RMS Titanic *was made there and the Cradley Heath women chainmakers' strike of 1910, called when the employers refused to pay a proposed minimum wage, was a landmark in industrial relations history.*

But in this tough area, where local culture includes such delicacies as faggots and peas and groaty pudding, a sense of humour has prevailed. The main protagonists of this Black Country wit have always been and indeed continue to be Enoch (pronounced Anock) and Eli (pronounced Ali). As many Black Country men served in the Great War, it should be no surprise that Enoch and Eli joined up together.

Black Country storyteller, Graham Langley, told the tale which follows to Taffy Thomas at Whitby Folk Festival in 2012.

Enoch and Eli stood knee-deep in mud and blood in a trench, sharing a Woodbine – or a 'coffin nail' as they called it.

Enoch reminded Eli that the good news was that the major had promised them a pound for every German they shot.

Enoch then told Eli that he didn't want to worry him, but the bad news was that there were £2,000 worth streaming across no-man's-land with fixed bayonets.

History doesn't recall Eli's response, although it's possible that the two pals' last words came quietly in the form of the following song:

> Take me back where the smoke blows black
> And the home-brewed ales flows free,
> And factory wenches line all the park benches,
> Cradley Heath means home to me.

However, due to the miracle of reincarnation allowed by the oral tradition, Enoch and Eli tales continue to thrive in this very special part of the Midlands.

Footnote

Before anyone wearing an anorak contacts us with the information that the song 'Cradley Heath means home to me' wasn't composed till the 1960s, we know; but as Enoch and Eli are a concept not constricted by any logical time frame, the authors are claiming a certain amount of poetic licence.

JACK'S WAGER

Throughout the 1970s, Taffy Thomas' folk theatre company, Magic Lantern, was fortunate to have as its lead singer the renowned Wolverhampton songwriter, Bill Caddick. Sometime during this period, Bill heard a story claiming that the song 'It's A Long Way To Tipperary', which was composed by Black Country variety artist Jack Judge in one night just prior to the outbreak of the First World War, was sung to win a bet in a pub. Bill turned this snippet into one of his finest songs, 'The Writing of Tipperary'. For this collection, Taffy has turned it back into a spoken word version.

The story begins with a family originating from Ireland. The communities that surround Birmingham, such as West Bromwich and Oldbury, have long provided sanctuary for immigrant Irish families fleeing the horrors of war and famine.

The family of Rodger Judge first came to the English Midlands from County Mayo in 1860. Eleven years later, in 1871, Rodger's youngest son, John Junior, married Mary McGuire in Oldbury. In 1872, their first child, John Thomas (known as Jack), was born and the family moved into Low Town near the Malt Shovel public house. Before long, Jack had two sisters: Jane-Ann and Mary.

Although the Judge family lived in poverty, Jack grew to be a big, striking, red-haired lad, tall and strong beyond his age. To help support his family, at the age of twelve Jack bluffed his way into a job with his father at Bromford Ironworks. Jack was popular, often whistling and always with a cheery quip or a ditty to sing.

In 1885, Jack and his father left the ironworks to become fish dealers. Together they opened a wet fish stall next to 'Polly on the Fountain', a drinking fountain opposite the Junction Vaults.

At that time, the main places of entertainment in Oldbury were the music halls – the Gaiety and the Old White Swan Museum and Concert Hall. Jack and Jane-Ann, his sister, sometimes went to the evening events at these venues, as well as to local public houses, to sell fish, cockles, mussels, whelks and prawns.

This Black Country tradition continued until the 1960s, when Taffy Thomas himself was resident in Dudley.

It was by watching the professionals at work during these visits to the halls that young Jack began to develop his own singing and comedy talent and he started to enter talent competitions. By the late 1890s, Jack Judge had become well known locally and was even offered some engagements further from home. However, Jack had to balance his entertainment ambitions against the survival of the family fish business, as his father had perished from TB at the age of thirty-eight.

As a grown man, Jack spent a lot of time in the Malt Shovel where the landlord's brother, Harry Williams (a disabled pianist), took time to write down and arrange Jack's songs. This was something Jack himself could not do, as he was virtually illiterate. In return, Jack promised Harry that if he ever got a song published, he would include his friend in the credits as co-author.

One night in the Malt Shovel, Jack was asked to oblige with a song. Accompanied by Harry, he launched into a tune called 'It's A Long Way To Connemara'.

A large Irish navvy, full of ale at the bar, seized Jack by the kerchief and muttered, 'I'll have you know, I'm a Tipperary man'.

Rather than get a bloody nose, Jack thought on his feet and came up with a new song. His friend Harry transcribed it as Jack was singing it, and then Jack put the words and music in a battered leather music case, which he took to all his performances.

When on tour to halls farther afield, Jack usually sought solace between shows in one of the local hostelries. He'd developed a scam. Easing the conversation around to his song-writing ability, he would bet strangers that he could compose a new song in one night and sing it at the next performance. He did this knowing that he had dozens of unused songs in that battered leather music case.

In January 1912, Jack was performing at the Grand Theatre in Stalybridge just east of Manchester. Being there for several nights, he was staying in a nearby pub and it was in that pub one evening that he pulled the song-in-a-night scam. Jack won five shillings when, on the 31 January, he sang 'It's A Long Way To Tipperary' – his new song!

Once out of that leather music case, the song began to fly. Other performers, including the famous music-hall star Florrie Forde, took it up and publisher Bert Feldman signed up the royalty in September 1912, adding another 'Long' to the title, and including Harry Williams as co-author of 'It's A Long, Long Way To Tipperary'.

The sheet music was billed as 'the marching anthem of the battlefields of Europe' and, within two years, nearly every serviceman marching off to the Great War knew it. Even at Armistice Day in 2013, the veterans marched past the Cenotaph in London still singing this tune. Just imagine what Jack Judge would have said had he known this when he won his five bob in 1912.

It's a Long, Long Way to Tipperary

Up to mighty London
Came an Irishman one day.
As the streets are paved with gold
Sure, everyone was gay,
Singing songs of Piccadilly,
Strand and Leicester Square,
Till Paddy got excited,
Then he shouted to them there:

It's a long way to Tipperary,
It's a long way to go.
It's a long way to Tipperary
To the sweetest girl I know!
Goodbye, Piccadilly,
Farewell, Leicester Square!
It's a long, long way to Tipperary,
But my heart's right there.

Paddy wrote a letter
To his Irish Molly-O,
Saying, 'Should you not receive it,
Write and let me know!'
'If I make mistakes in spelling,
Molly, dear,' said he,
'Remember, it's the pen that's bad,
Don't lay the blame on me!'

It's a long way to Tipperary,
It's a long way to go.
It's a long way to Tipperary
To the sweetest girl I know!
Goodbye, Piccadilly,
Farewell, Leicester Square!
It's a long, long way to Tipperary,
But my heart's right there.

Molly wrote a neat reply
To Irish Paddy-O,
Saying 'Mike Maloney
Wants to marry me, and so
Leave the Strand and Piccadilly
Or you'll be to blame,
For love has fairly drove me silly:
Hoping you're the same!'

It's a long way to Tipperary,
It's a long way to go.
It's a long way to Tipperary
To the sweetest girl I know!
Goodbye, Piccadilly,
Farewell, Leicester Square!
It's a long, long way to Tipperary,
But my heart's right there.

Jack Judge and Harry Williams (1912)

Five

When Truth Becomes Legend

THE TALE OF THE ACCRINGTON PALS

Whether the various sightings of heavenly visions on the battlefields of Belgium and France, such as the Angels of Mons, were real or fantasy, we shall never know. The following ghostly tale, however, is inspired by true events and is well known throughout East Lancashire.

The 11th (Service) Battalion of the East Lancashire regiment, known as the Accrington Pals, suffered badly in the Battle of the Somme, losing 80 per cent of their men on the first day of the battle. So by the end of the war, the battle-weary survivors among them were glad to be making their way north to Le Havre for demobolisation.

But their suffering had not ended yet, for the winter of 1918–19 was particularly harsh, and as they battled against the elements this particular group of Lancashire men found themselves in a tight spot and under a last bout of heavy fire. Pinned down in their trench, their losses were mounting and the few that were left were about to give up hope when, in the fog of battle, they saw several greyish figures standing beckoning them to safety.

Shaking, yet certain these figures were angels and meant them no harm, the soldiers followed the strangers who, sure enough, led them to sanctuary in a nearby monastery.

As their panic subsided, the soldiers saw that their rescuers were not real angels after all, but were nonetheless holy, for they were Benedictine monks, dressed in their grey habits.

The soldiers remained hidden in the monastery for several days, resting and recovering from their wounds, and the monks looked after them well. They fed the soldiers good food and gave them a special drink that they made, called Benedictine.

When the soldiers were strong once more, they made their way out of the monastery, discovering that they were now only a short distance from the safety of Le Havre. While waiting to be shipped home, the soldiers headed for a local bar where, over a glass of the monks' famous, warming Benedictine drink, they shared the details of their rescue from the trench, only to discover that the monastery they

believed they had been taken to – and the monks who they believed had led them there – had been wiped out in the French Revolution.

The soldiers never forgot the moment that their lives had been saved by the ghosts of those kind holy men and they never forgot the sweet liqueur which had helped to heal their bodies.

And if you go into the Miner's Club in Burnley, do not be surprised if you see one of its members ordering a pint of bitter and a 'Bene 'n' 'ot' chaser – a shot of Benedictine mixed with hot water and lemon or grapefruit juice.

KEEPING A PROMISE TO THE KAISER

The following tale is based on a true event that was brought to light recently by historian Richard van Emden. Van Emden was carrying out some research for his book Meeting the Enemy: The Human Face of the Great War *(Bloomsbury, 2013) when he came across some surprising correspondence between the Foreign Office and the German Government. The correspondence, which included an official memorandum, centred on a British prisoner of war named Captain Robert Campbell, who had been leading the 1st Battalion of the East Surrey Regiment in the fighting at the Mons-Condé Canal, which ran across the border between France and Belgium.*

The historian was looking for case studies involving German and British people having personal contact during the war. He was hoping their stories would give him a better insight into the true feelings that people on opposing sides had towards one another. He was fascinated in particular by surprising stories of chivalry, of people showing unexpected compassion towards one another or abiding by unwritten rules of decency amid all the brutality and chaos. Captain Robert Campbell's story appeared to be a perfect example.

Among the 100,000 soldiers in the British Expeditionary Force who were the first to arrive in France at the start of the war was twenty-nine-year-old Captain Robert Campbell. An experienced soldier with eleven years of army service already under his belt, Captain Campbell was duly selected as leader of the first of eighteen battalions from the East Surrey Regiment who marched off to defend their country. He and his men did not have to wait long to prove their mettle, for just weeks into the war, they were dug firmly into a defensive position on the banks of the Mons-Condé Canal, about to take part in their country's first major battle of the Great War.

Just after dawn on 23 August 1914, the Battle of Mons began. Captain Campbell and his battalion fought bravely, but the size of their enemy's force was overwhelming and by nightfall they were forced to start retreating. The Germans were not going to let them escape easily, and maintained a heavy assault. All through the night and into the next day, the British soldiers fought a desperate rearguard action, but their casualties were heavy and Captain Campbell was among them. Seriously injured, he was unable to follow as his men made their retreat and he had no choice but to let himself be captured.

Luckily for the captain, Germany was among the forty-four nations who, in 1907, had been willing to sign an agreement promising to treat all prisoners of war humanely. So thanks to this agreement – which if we were speaking more formally would be referred to as the Hague Convention – the captain was not allowed to suffer beyond the indignity of capture and was soon taken to a military hospital in Cologne, where his wounds were treated.

Healed and healthy once more, he was then transported across Germany to the prisoner-of-war camp in Magdeburg. To any soldier, trained to fight and keen to do his part for his country, the prospect of languishing in a prisoner-of-war camp must have been excruciating, and Captain Campbell was no exception. But there were two long years of incarceration to follow in that Magdeburg jail before the officer could taste the sweet air on the other side of the perimeter fence. And when his chance to leave did come, it was in extraordinary circumstances.

In the autumn of 1916, more than twenty-four months since he had been wounded at Mons, Captain Campbell received a letter from home. His dear mother, Louise, was dying of cancer.

Finding themselves in Captain Campbell's shoes, many men may have accepted that he had seen the last of her. But not Robert. He requested pen and paper and wrote to the one person he believed might have the power to help him. He wrote to the Kaiser himself, Wilhelm II, and he begged him to allow an upstanding British officer the chance to see his dying mother one last time.

Now, for all his aggressive ambition for his country, Kaiser Bill was not an uncompassionate man. He could never find it in himself to despise Britain completely, for while it was a nation with which he was at war, it was also a nation with which he was inextricably linked through his mother's bloodline. So whether it was because Campbell's letter appealed to his sense of family fidelity, whether he admired the plucky captain's resourcefulness in writing to him, or whether he simply made a decision on a whim, the Kaiser promptly granted the British officer two weeks' compassionate leave. But there was a condition. The Kaiser expected his generosity to be repaid with honesty and the captain's leave was to be granted solely on the condition that he promise faithfully to return.

Astounded by the Kaiser's show of chivalry, Captain Campbell duly swore an oath on his honour to make his way back to Magdeburg once his visit had ended.

Without delay, a telegram from Berlin was despatched to London, announcing: 'Capt R.C. Campbell is arriving at Gravesend on 7 November on a fortnight's leave of absence on parole.' The surprised captain swiftly set off on a two-day journey home, travelling by train through Holland and then by boat across the sea to Blighty.

On 7 November, as the telegram had predicted, he arrived by his sick mother's bedside back home in Gravesend in Kent.

Captain Campbell spent one last precious week with his mother before the time came for him to keep his promise to the Kaiser and return to his German prison.

Not once did he consider breaking the oath he had taken. Not once did his superiors suggest that he should. For everyone accepted that the Kaiser's gesture of kindness should be met with respect.

So it was that Captain Robert Campbell made his way back to port and boarded a return passage to Holland, crossing that country once again by train into Germany.

If Captain Campbell's arrival back at the prison gate surprised his captors, his attempted escape soon after must have surprised them all the more.

For why would a man who had been given his key to freedom throw it away only to try to break out the hard way, spending nine hard months digging a tunnel? But, being a man with a strong sense of duty, that was precisely what Campbell did. Sadly, though, his efforts were to no avail, as he and his three fellow escapees were captured just over the border into Holland and dragged back to their cells.

In the months and years that followed, the captain would try to make other attempts at escape, but each of them were equally unsuccessful and eventually he had to accept that his contribution to the war was over. He was not to leave Magdeburg again until the Armistice was signed. When he finally made it home to Gravesend once more, Louise Campbell's bed was empty, for having seen her beloved son, she had finally lost her battle with cancer in February 1917.

Captain Campbell may have missed out on the bulk of the fighting in the First World War, but he would have his chance to serve his country again in 1939, when he rejoined the army to serve in the Royal Observer Corps on the Isle of Wight in the Second World War.

Once again, the gods appeared to look down favourably upon him, for Campbell survived everything that the war threw at him. He saw peace restored to British shores, and remained on the Isle of Wight for the rest of his life, refusing to let his light go out until 1966 and not before he had reached the grand old age of eighty-one.

THE POPPY LADY

On 2 May 1915, Lieutenant Alexis Helmer was killed by a German artillery shell in the Second Battle of Ypres. He was a friend and former student of the military doctor Lieutenant Colonel John McCrae. Both men served in the Canadian army. The following day, after leading the burial service and while sitting near to his friend's grave, McCrae wrote the lines to a poem which has become emblematic of the First World War: 'In Flanders Fields'.

McCrae's powerful poem was first published in the Punch *magazine in December 1915. Three years later, in November 1918, it was also printed in the American publication known as the* Ladies' Home Journal, *and it was here that a lady named Moina Belle Michael first*

came upon it. Inspired by the poem, Moina began to
promote the idea of wearing poppies for remembrance –
a tradition which has lasted to this day and is central to
The Royal British Legion's annual Poppy Appeal which
raises millions of pounds every year. This is Moina's story.

There is an Ancient Roman legend about Ceres, the corn goddess, who was so exhausted from her search for her lost daughter, Proserpine, that all the corn in the land stopped growing. To help her to rest, Somnus, the god of sleep, created the poppy, the seeds of which he blended with honey and milk and offered to Ceres as a drink to soothe her to sleep. While the goddess slept, the corn began to grow again and when she woke, she could see stretched before her miles of cornfields, sprinkled with red, like drops of blood.

From that day forwards, not only did people believe that corn poppies – also called corn roses – had to be present for a good corn harvest to grow, they also believed that the poppy could bring about merciful sleep.

Poppies began to spring up as symbol of sleep in life and death in legends all over the world and throughout time. Then came the First World War and it was while working as a surgeon in the field hospitals in France that one soldier was so struck by the abundance of this bright red flower – which covered the battlefields and seemed to spring from the blood-drenched soil onto which so many soldiers fell – that he put pen to paper and wrote a poem which was destined to be famous. His name was John McRae and his poem was 'In Flanders Fields'.

But the story does not stop there …

One day in 1918, while helping to host a conference in the War Office in New York, an American lady, Moina Belle Michael, decided to take a short break. She found a quiet spot, picked up a magazine and began to leaf through it. She noticed that one of the pages was marked, and casting her eye over it, she was immediately struck by a powerful image which was printed alongside a short poem. The picture showed three soldiers, rising into the air like angels ascending to heaven, above a ground strewn with wooden crosses and poppy flowers.

Then Moina read the poem, finding herself profoundly moved by words which had clearly been written from the heart on the battlefields of Belgium three years before by a man called Lieutenant Colonel John McCrae.

This was 'In Flanders Fields', and as Moina read each verse, she felt as if the voices of all the dead soldiers from those battlefields were speaking directly to her.

> If ye break faith with us who die
> We shall not sleep, though poppies grow

Moina knew that she could never provide a true representation of what those brave soldiers had done on the Western Front but she could, as the poem said, keep the faith and carry the torch for those who had paid the ultimate sacrifice. Right there, she made a promise that from that day on, she would always wear a poppy as a sign of remembrance.

She sealed her promise in writing, by hastily scribbling her own poem in reply to McCrae's, on a crumpled, yellowed envelope which had been lying on her desk.

Just as she finished the last line, a man who was attending the conference in the War Office approached Moina. Thanking her for her hard work, he gave her a ten dollar cheque.

Moina thanked the man and, rising from her chair, she told him that she knew what to buy with the money and that she was going shopping right away. 'I shall buy red poppies,' she announced with a bright smile, 'twenty-five red poppies.' Then she showed the man the poem and explained to him her pledge.

The man spread the word and, as the day went on, all the delegates at the conference – one after the next – came to see Moina to ask for a poppy for their buttonhole.

Moina quickly ran out of fresh poppies, which set her thinking: if the poppies were a symbol of remembrance, then surely it would be better if they never faded.

She set off on a quest all over New York City, looking for artificial versions of the blood-red flower. Finally, after hours of searching, she found what she was looking for. Sitting among the flowers in Wanamaker's famous department store were two-dozen perfect, red silk poppies, each with four petals – just like the field poppies of Flanders.

Word of Moina's remembrance poppies began to spread and the demand grew. When she ran out of silk poppies, she made some more, and some more … until she had made so many, she became known far and wide as 'The Poppy Lady'. She had sown the seeds of the Flanders Fields Memorial Poppy and had created a worldwide symbol of remembrance.

In Flanders Fields

In Flanders fields the poppies blow
Between the crosses, row on row,
That mark our place; and in the sky
The larks, still bravely singing, fly
Scarce heard amid the guns below.

We are the Dead. Short days ago
We lived, felt dawn, saw sunset glow,
Loved and were loved, and now we lie
In Flanders fields.

Take up our quarrel with the foe:
To you from failing hands we throw
The torch; be yours to hold it high.
If ye break faith with us who die
We shall not sleep, though poppies grow
In Flanders fields.

Lt Col John McCrae (1872–1918)

About the
Authors

Taffy Thomas MBE trained as a literature and drama teacher at Dudley College of Education and taught for several years in Wolverhampton. He founded and directed the legendary folk theatre company, Magic Lantern, and founded and directed the rural community arts company, Charivari, with their popular touring unit, the Fabulous Salami Brothers, which he fronted and performed in until he was sidelined by a stroke, aged just thirty-six. He turned back to storytelling as self-imposed speech therapy. Taffy has a repertoire of more than 300 stories and tales collected mainly from traditional oral sources, and is now the most experienced English storyteller, having pioneered many storytelling residencies and appeared at the National Storytelling Festival in the USA and the Bergen Arts Festival in Norway. In the 2001 New Year Honours List he was awarded the MBE for services to storytelling and charity and, in the same year, performed for the Blue Peter Prom at the Royal Albert Hall. In October 2009, Taffy accepted the honorary position of the first Laureate for Storytelling. He is currently artistic director of Tales in Trust, the Northern Centre for Storytelling, in Grasmere. He tours nationally and internationally, working in both entertainment and education and is a patron of the Society for Storytelling. In October 2013, Taffy was selected as Outstanding Male Storyteller in the British Awards for Storytelling Excellence.

Helen Watts is a writer, editor and publisher who has worked in educational publishing for twenty-six years, the majority of those specialising in the production of literacy resources for teachers and children at primary school level. Her experience includes magazine and book publishing, and she has worked for some of the biggest and best publishing houses in the UK, including Scholastic and Heinemann Educational. For ten years, Helen was editor of the *Literacy Time* magazine, after which she founded The Literacy Club, through which she published magazines and books, including the paperback collection *Taffy's Coat Tales* by Taffy Thomas MBE. May 2013 saw the publication of Helen's first historical fiction novel, *One Day In Oradour* (A&C Black/Bloomsbury), which received a nomination for the 2014 CILIP Carnegie Medal for an outstanding book for children and young adults. Her second novel, *No Stone Unturned*, will be published by A&C Black/Bloomsbury in 2014. Helen's recent educational publications include *WWI Primary Teaching Resource – Facts, activities and pictures on The Great War*, *Make Phonics Fun* and *Building Blocks: Themed Activities for the Early Years Foundation Stage* (all published by LCP).